FULL CIRCLE

Building resilience in business and life from the jagged edges of PTSD

JO HASSAN

Reviews...

"Being the remarkable woman that she is, Jo's own observations and experiences have provided her with a unique capacity to offer valuable insights to others facing difficulties be they in life, relationships or business."
Dr Tom George, Psychiatrist

"This book could be the catalyst you need to make some positive changes in life if you are affected by any mental health issues, particularly if they are impacting on your work life ... had me engaged from the start to the very end: a powerful read!"
"...a powerful personal story about the real struggles of dealing with PTSD and mental health issues."
Bill Blaikie Lieutenant Colonel (Retired), MNZM,
Author and PTSD Advocate

"Full Circle is an honest and raw account of determination and resilience despite the circumstances. The personal insight into PTSD and useful strategies into pushing through when the going gets tough is an inspiring read for all."
Martin Brooker, Commodore (Retired), CSC, RANR,
Founder and Director Quench Group

"An engaging narrative of personal and professional development. Jo Hassan relates how, in responding to adversity, a resilient self evolves."
Michael Finn, Michael Finn Health Services

"I loved that this book is so conversational."
Kim Skubris, MC, Coach, Journalist

"We won't 'heal' PTSD by looking away from it, but perhaps we make a good start by looking at it, and then through it for a solution. And in this book Jo has the courage to do just that!"
Julie Cross CSP, Professional Speaker and Author

"Jo is the epitome of resilience and walks her talk.
Whether you're a business owner, leader, parent, spouse or friend, Jo's experiences provide insight into her genius of rising above your circumstances to create a life and business full of life energy and vitality. Even better is that you get to learn how you can too."
Jane Anderson CSP,
Personal Branding Expert and Author

"...an endearing story of surviving and overcoming adversity to thrive in the world."
Sally Foley-Lewis, Productive Leadership Speaker,
Author and Mentor

"...a 'warts and all' account of one woman's journey through life and business."
Susan M Green, Founder Verdant QBooks,
Bookkeeper, Writer, Health Practitioner

"Jo, you have an absolutely incredible story. Thank you for sharing so many personal and challenging moments in your life... I have such admiration for you and I'm inspired by your courage and brilliance. YOU ARE AMAZING!!!!!"
Karen Jacobsen, The GPS Girl, Voice of Siri, Speaker,
Singer, Author

"Jo shares the story of life – the ups, the downs, the hopes, the doubts and the realisation that we are here to experience it all."
Chris Wildeboer, Founder of Balance Central,
Author and Speaker

"An inspiring book which I hope helps other people who are suffering or who have suffered from PTSD, postnatal depression, depression or other challenges."
Paula Tripp, Jo's Loving Sister

"A heart-warming read..."
Daryl Elliott Green, twiceshot.com

"Keep wearing pink, keep smiling."
Margie Patterson

Copyright ©2019 Jo Hassan, All Rights Reserved.

Except for the purposes of reviewing, no part of this publication may be reproduced or transmitted in any form or by any means, electronic or mechanical, including photocopying, recording or any information storage or retrieval system, without the written permission of the author. Infringers of copyright render themselves liable for prosecution.

Disclaimer: Every effort has been made to ensure this book is as accurate and complete as possible, however there may be errors both typographical and in content. The author and the publisher shall not be held liable or responsible to any person or entity with respect to any loss or damage caused or alleged to have been caused directly or indirectly by the information contained in this book.

ISBN: 978-0-6482169-1-9
Published by: PinkWise®
                   PO Box 1015 Stafford QLD 4053 Australia
Cover Design: Catucci Design
Illustrations: Brand by Design

Medical Disclaimer

This work represents the personal experience and opinions of the author and as such should not be taken as medical treatment or advice. The reader assumes all risk for any actions taken based on the content or comments in this book. The author bears no responsibility for omissions or errors; the text and illustrations are intended as a general commentary only, and are not to be considered comprehensive in any way. It is advised that each person seek competent and current advice from qualified health professionals.

Dedicated to my family. For without them this story would have a very different beginning, middle and ending.

Some names have been changed and other non-critical details altered to protect the identity of people mentioned. While every effort has been made to recall past events accurately, the memories contained within this book are the author's own and may differ from those of others.

Contents

Reviews 3

Introduction 11

1: Karma Chameleon 13

2: The Girl from 'The Village' 17

3: The Man from the Divided Island 25

4: From 'Concord' to 'The In Crowd' to Tropical Queensland. 33

5: The Backpacker's Whirlwind Romance 43

6: The Man in the Village 53

7: A Wedding, Times Two 59

8: "*You* will make or break this family" 65

9: Incompetent Mother 77

10: *Shhhhh!* Don't Tell Anyone! 87

11: Working Through It 97
12: A Star is Born – But It's Not as Shiny as it Could Be 107
13: Becoming PinkWise® 117
14: The Queen of Resilience 129
15: "I Am What I Choose To Become" 137
Epilogue - Full Circle, Times Two 141
Jo's Recovery Reading and Listening 151
Other Books Referenced 157
Jo's Recovery Summary 159
Cultural Translation and Other Notes 163
Endnotes 165
Acknowledgements 169
About Jo Hassan 173

Introduction

When I started to write this book, I thought I was going to write something quite different. But I sat down and began to plot out what I really wanted to say, and by the end of a very intensive planning session, this is what emerged as the project I wanted to devote my time to first. I know there will be other books I'm going to write, but this is what I wanted to share the most. First.

This is not your usual business book. This is the back story on the back story.

Because post-traumatic stress disorder[i] (PTSD) has shaped most of my adult life, I want to help people understand that this is not something relative only to first responders, the military and people affected by armed conflict. It's also not something only found among survivors of abuse and 'obvious' trauma. It's far bigger than that. And my own journey towards, through, and mostly out the other side – hey I'm still evolving here – is what I know others can learn from.

As part of my business focus from 2006 to now, I have spent a lot of time developing coping strategies and helpful options for exhausted stressed out business owners, executives and busy people. This book then is an unabashed chance to share how that works for those I coach to develop themselves and their businesses. Because business is about people first. My PEPP® coaching programs for small business owners or individual leaders stem from everything I've learned about building robust resilience and coping with the unexpected. I'm excited to have this chance to introduce them through my personal stories of 'how I got this far' in 'one PinkWise® piece'.

This tome has helped me to fulfil a dream I've always had to write a book, and in the end it was unexpectedly very cathartic. A bonus is sharing my story with my family who previously didn't know much of what I was going through. It's not necessarily what I would advocate as a plan today but thirty years ago, from the other side of the world, it was much easier to protect them from hurting whilst I hurt.

So I'm now hoping that you the reader will find my story interesting, and helpful. I invite you inside to take a journey with me on getting through life and to come back around to your own full circle.

1: Karma Chameleon

Everyone has times in their lives when they feel the need to re-group either as the result of a carefully crafted plan that goes wrong or, as in my case 'back then', because my whole world was caving in. Every time I hear the song "Karma Chameleon" by Culture Club I'm reminded of that time. And it happened again recently.

I was attending a women's retreat in Kandanga in the beautiful Mary Valley in Queensland's Sunshine Coast Hinterland. In our pre-weekend preparations we were to have submitted our favourite song which for me is "Dancing Queen" by Abba. When Karma Chameleon was played as background music during an activity I had to ask our facilitator Vickie "Whose favourite song is this?" She replied "No one's – this is a happy playlist".

So there you go! The song that for the last thirty-four years I've affectionately referred to as my 'disaster song', was played because for others it's happy! Not that I didn't enjoy the song – I did – it was just the circumstances around it...

It was September 1983 and I was travelling in the car with Pa[1]. He was with me because I had failed *yet another* driving test. I had also just failed all my 'A Level'[2] school exams, so would not be going to university as I had hoped and been planning for. *And* I had just been dropped by my first boyfriend Edward.

Karma Chameleon came on the radio. It was number one in the UK Singles Chart where it stayed for six weeks and was actually the biggest selling single of the year. Clearly I was not the only person who enjoyed singing along to it. So I lamented everything wrong with my life at that time and Pa went into a philosophical discussion along the lines of the famous Abraham Lincoln speech[ii] "and this too shall pass".

But what has really stood in my mind were his further comments along the lines of having music associations for different times in my life, as he did, hence Karma Chameleon being my 'disaster song' even though I actually like it.

When I think back, there have been a number of occasions when I've experienced 'situational depression'[iii] including as a result of protracted difficult situations in business.

---

1 Dad.
2 General Certificate of Education (GCE) Advanced Level (A Level) is a secondary school leaving qualification in the UK.

Now that's a quite different 'animal' to clinical depression[iv], postnatal depression[v] (PND) or post-traumatic stress disorder (PTSD) which were the foundations for writing this book. At the time though, the pain was very real, just perhaps not so long-lasting and completely debilitating.

As I share my journey of a vibrant life with sometimes shockingly jagged edges, I hope you find something in my story that is helpful and/or relevant to you or someone who is important to you.

Yes, I really did move from The English Village to The Land Down Under via a relationship with a Turkish Cypriot man who brought more than just cultural diversity to my life! Sometimes I can recall *exactly* how I felt in some of the more unusual situations I found myself. At other times, I know the event happened - in some cases I have the original notes I made along the way – and a stoic British 'stiff upper lip'[vi] has quelled the feeling or perhaps therapy at the time (or later) buried the memory.

There's a funny 'villagism'[3] to not "do or say anything you wouldn't want your parrot to repeat to the village gossip". There are a lot of 'don't let the parrot see or hear stories' here because it's time to start the conversation around a number of supposedly taboo subjects.

Now that I'm all grown up I'm ready to share, and start a conversation with you that I hope inspires you to start a conversation with others. That may be to seek the help that you have been too embarrassed to ask for or suggest

---

3   A 'Jo-ism' meaning funny thing said about a village.

someone you care about takes action. Or simply so that you can say "Yes – I get this. I have felt the same way".

Or perhaps to defy the myth that once you're down you have to stay down every day forever. It is possible to 'grow' or strengthen your resilience. But you might need help. Notice the ride you're on and take steps to adjust the vehicle as you hit speed bumps and road blocks along the way.

Additionally I trust you'll have a giggle at some of the absurdly funny coincidences that have made me laugh at myself and the universe along the way.

Everything really is in perfect order!

2: The Girl from 'The Village'

When I was growing up I had no idea at all that I was living in the "classic English village". Fulmer[vii] in the county of Buckinghamshire is just twenty miles from the city of London, yet we had a stream running down the end of the garden, which was actually the River Alderbourne, as well as sheep just the other side of it.

There was one pub (The Black Horse or simply "The Black"), one church, one village hall, one tiny shop incorporating a post office, one tiny school, a cricket field and a horse stud. Houses ranged from tiny terrace cottages to multi-million dollar mansions with armed guards. My parents are still living in the same detached house I grew up in. It was simply a village five miles from the larger town of Slough[4] [viii] where they both grew up.

---

4   A light industrial town with lots of factories including for Mars bars so there is often a rich chocolate aroma in the air. It was the scene of a popular television satirical comedy "The Office".

Whilst 'the parentals'[5] aren't really religious, I was baptised in St James Church and was a founding attendee of 'The Beehive' playgroup in the village hall. I considered the pub just to be a place for playing after school, because I was friends with the publican's daughters. As I grew up, the hall also hosted 'Youth Club' – a weekly hangout for young teenagers to play pinball, suck on a lollipop with a packet of crisps and generally keep out of mischief. The once a term disco was a highlight and I can remember being fascinated by the lighting show! The hall was also 'pinked up' for my 21st birthday party.

During my lifetime, the village has grown in popularity amongst the rich and famous so it is not uncommon to see extravagant cars and Hollywood stars at the pub who consider themselves 'local'. A number of factors have contributed to this: it is close to London's Heathrow Airport, Pinewood Studios (renowned for thousands of movies including all James Bond and Harry Potter) is in the next village, and there is now convenient access to the M25 (the motorway ring road that circumnavigates London) and the M40 to Oxford. Nicole Kidman called herself a local when she and her adopted family lived in the village during the time she was married to Tom Cruise.

Other famous people who crossed my path because they lived in another neighbouring village called Denham were Cilla Black and Sir John and Lady Mills. They were amongst the 'normal' well-known customers whilst I worked my first real job in nearby Gerrards Cross, which the locals referred

---

5   A 'Jo-ism' nickname for 'parents'.

to as simply 'GX'. It was a wine and spirits 'off-licence' with a comprehensive delicatessen selling a very wide range of cheeses, cured meats and other food items. One Sunday lunchtime comes to mind when Cilla, with a basket full of goods to be put through my cash register, allowed a couple of young girls to go ahead of her because they were only buying one item. They knew who she was and were completely star-struck and appreciative of her kindness.

Filming for movies was a regular occurrence. I remember the day they filmed the "Going home from the airport" scene at the start of International Velvet[ix] (1978). I wasn't born though when the 'Watersplash' was featured in Genevieve[x] (1953). The Watersplash is where the River Alderbourne literally flows across the road. To me it was where I rode my bicycle for tadpole collection and to Pa it was a place he used to keep a brush hidden to wash his motorbike when it got muddy!

The school had two classrooms and in the time I was there a demountable was installed where we went for lunch. It was the era of milk at morning break and a cooked meal in the middle of the day. After lunch we played traditional games like hopscotch, elastics or British Bulldog.

Several memories are etched on my brain and I'm delighted that in recent years courtesy of Facebook, I've reconnected with three people from this school who I knew when I was five years old: Christine, Tony and Peter. Christine was famous for giving me a 'free haircut'. It all happened so quickly I hardly knew what was going on. She said "Let's play hairdressers", grabbed a pair of scissors and started cutting!

Luckily she randomly grabbed some hair from underneath. It was a miracle Ma[6] didn't notice on the day.

That all changed once we went to the 'real' hairdresser though, as she pulled Ma aside and said "Look at this. Someone else has been cutting and to make it look nice I'll have go even shorter myself". It was the worst haircut of my life and made me feel I looked like a boy. Thank goodness (for once) for the homemade 'girly' frocks because I recall being so unhappy looking masculine as I struggled to grow into my femininity.

I didn't realise it at the time but this was the era of corporal punishment. Once my next-door neighbour Stephen, put our teacher Mrs Wade's makeup in the fish tank. Yes. He went to her handbag, took out the makeup purse and put it in the fish tank! I can't recall the repercussions of that but I do remember a boy getting whacked on the backside with a shoe by the headmaster, Mr Duncan. Another memory from my next school was of another boy having to take off his own belt and then being told to lean over and the teacher hit him with it.

A variation of this punishment happened sometimes at home. Whilst my home life was generally calm and loving, there was the day when my ballet teacher Mrs French came closer to me to inspect 'something' on my thigh and it was an impression of Ma's hand showing red through my thick pale pink ballet tights! Goodness knows what I did to

---

6   Mum.

deserve that. Perhaps, just not wanting to go to ballet and not cooperating with getting ready.

There were seven years of mixed emotion around ballet, then tap and modern dance lessons. With hindsight I'm really glad Ma pushed me to dance as a life skill but it wasn't something I cherished at the time, especially the exams. Although I absolutely love dancing now – and have even had some lessons recently – back then it didn't seem like it needed to be something that ran in the family so that I could take after my paternal Grandmother.

After a colourful childhood on the stage as a dancer, Pa's Mum Connie (who we affectionately called Maxie) settled in Tottenham in London and worked in a bakery. Not just any bakery though, the one closest to the stadium that the famed Tottenham Hotspur football team called home. In the days before nutritionists and the regime of strict diets, she would complete the morning/afternoon tea cake orders for the soccer players.

She didn't fall for any of those handsome young men though, but rather a guy called Sid from the neighbouring bicycle shop, who became a clever motorcycle mechanic. He was the 'right hand man' of a famous speed demon called Herbert (Bert) Le Vack[xi] who was the first motorcycle rider to break the elusive 100 miles per hour around Brooklands Race Track. He was a world speed record holder, throughout the 1920s.

Sid and Maxie's regular mode of transport was a motorcycle and sidecar and in 1924 Sid opened a motorcycle dealership in Slough. Unfortunately Sid died around the time I was born so I never met him to give him a more endearing name. By then though, Pa was also a keen motorcyclist and represented the UK in several forms of motorcycle sport, especially endurance trials. He still has the Barbours[7] [xii] hanging in the garage at home from when he was a member of the International Six Days Trials Team[xiii].

So Pa naturally took over the family business and had two daughters!

My sister Paula is two and half years younger than me and we mostly played well as children until we became teenagers. Then the fighting started which was sometimes physical! I don't remember much about this but do recall lots of arguments with Ma over just about everything. I guess that was some sort of 'rite of passage'.

We spent most weekends of our childhood at motorcycle events where Pa was officiating. Sometimes it was so boring sitting in the car waiting and playing endless games of hangman[8]. Sometimes though at trials[xiv,] we were actually allowed to help with the scoring. At other times, especially as I became older, I was in awe of special situations we found ourselves in. For example when I had a 'teen crush' on Barry Sheene[xv] it was really easy for Pa to arrange for me to meet him and get his autograph!

On several other occasions we were in the VIP box next to the start line for the British Grand Prix[xvi] at Silverstone.

---

7   Classic waxed cotton clothing for inclement weather.
8   Hangman is a paper and pencil guessing game.

These were exciting times for the girl from The Village. I can remember being fascinated at the privilege of watching the race so close to the motorbikes yet they were going so fast (in the middle of the straight) that you couldn't read the numbers and only knew who they were by watching the live television screen!

Despite the era, having daughters didn't stop Pa encouraging us to ride motorcycles... a little bit. From time to time he'd bring home a couple of kids' bikes that we'd ride around the huge apple tree in the back garden: round and round. The same apple tree with the swing he'd made. We had hours and hours of fun on it throughout our childhood. The same swing that caused Paula to have her first stitches when cousin Charlie pushed the seat with no one on and the wooden seat hit her just above the eye!

Bicycles were different. Paula and I rode our bicycles 'down the lane' to the woods and around the village all the time. Sometimes we'd be out for many hours.

I didn't realise it at the time but my family life was really pretty special. It was lovely when Maxie came for Sunday lunch – which was always a roast meat with lots of vegetables – and I'd marvel at the contents of her handbag. The contents of any woman's handbag are fascinating but I've never met anyone else who carried a dictionary! Along with the snuff, Fisherman's Friend lollies (if you can call them lollies!), lipstick, lip brush and lip liner etc, she carried the ability to look up a word... and then joked that it was hard to do so, when you didn't already know how to spell it.

After lunch Paula, Maxie and I would play Canasta[9] or Monopoly. We were very competitive and I treasure that some scoring notes are the still in the card box to this day. The games were even more spirited at Christmas time when my cousins Charlie and Gemma were there too! Around the (sometimes epic) tournaments we children had great fun sneaking food in serviettes that we'd later share at a secret midnight feast in our shared bedroom.

When we went to Maxie's house we always enjoyed the Mr Kipling French Fancies[10] and that she had a hot water bottle. To this day I think of Maxie every time I use a hot water bottle: she taught me how to 'burp' it or squeeze the air out.

We called Ma's parents Nana and Grandad and trips to their home were not complete without sneaking to the lolly tin in the sideboard for a mint fondant or Mint Cracknel[11] or a visit to the greenhouse down the garden to collect produce to take home. Paula and I enjoyed helping to gather beans, raspberries and other goodies. We often brought rhubarb back to The Village too and Ma would make the most delicious rhubarb and orange meringue hot pudding with it.

Whilst I led a mostly idyllic childhood in The Village, the man who was to become my husband had already grown up and 'run away'- to the other side of the world.

---

9   A card game in the rummy family with two packs of cards.
10 Tiny sponge cakes with vanilla fondant then covered in icing.
11 A crisp mint candy like shards of glass covered in chocolate. It has been unavailable in the UK for many years. It is however available in every supermarket in Australia as 'Mint Crisp' and I always take twenty bars to Paula when I return to The Village.

3: The Man from the Divided Island

Veli was born in Larnaca, Cyprus, whilst it was still part of the British Empire. A sense of uneasiness was in the air though and his parents made a decision to flee to London via Turkey. There was violence in Cyprus through the 1950s and '60s and a coup d'état[xvii] in 1974 divided the island between Greece and Turkey.

Veli's dad, Semir went first to find a job, which he did at a tannery in Highbury in London. For an illiterate man who was pulled out of school to work at age seven - climbing palm trees to harvest coconuts - he was never out of work. You wouldn't meet a more gentle soul: a kind man with simple taste who would give away his last dollar or the shirt on his back, if he believed someone else's need was greater than his.

Veli and his Mum Hareem followed to London after a year. Veli was immediately immersed in school even though he didn't speak English and found his love of all sport helped him settle in.

Whilst Semir was from a village in Cyprus, Hareem was from a more 'moneyed' upbringing on the Greek Island of Kos and had more sophisticated tastes in everything. Going back a generation or two though, the wealth was perhaps sourced unscrupulously: apparently from pirates! It was a miracle Semir and Hareem came together and when they fell in love, they went to great lengths to stay a couple. There was always confusion around her birthday as she was born on 29th February but further to that, she was too young to be married, so somehow lied about her age. Throughout her life this filtered through, even to passports and got us into family trouble when, sixty plus years on, we inadvertently gave her an eightieth birthday card in the 'wrong' year!

Unfortunately, Semir had a workplace accident and seriously injured his arm. This wasn't all bad however. Even though it was the 1950s, he received compensation that was enough money for the deposit to purchase a sizeable home. It was on three levels and at the end of a terrace next to Highbury Park. Hareem was a talented seamstress and did 'piece work' from home, so one room was devoted to an industrial sewing machine, overlocker and other equipment.

The Hassan family occupied the top floor and other rooms and floors were rented out to supplement their income. 'Strangers' or at least people who weren't family or friends living under the same roof led to some different scenarios from all the families I knew. For example, the fridge had a padlock on it!

After getting his head around learning English (to me he always sounded like a cockney) Veli did well at school, excelling in mathematics and technical drawing. School was quite strict; many times he told the story of getting the cane for running on the wrong side of an empty corridor. It was empty because he'd forgotten a book and went back to his locker to collect it after the class had started. Unfortunately, the headmaster happened to be walking down the same corridor and he'd broken a rule.

There were numerous rules at his home too and sometimes the punishment was being hung upside down from a swing. I could never fathom how a mother could do that to a son, as it seemed more like torture to me than the more conventional forms of corporal punishment I'd been exposed to.

Living next to Highbury Park gave Veli a huge backyard in which to kick his beloved soccer ball. He was actually really good. Good enough to be selected for Arsenal's junior team! Hareem though encouraged him away from a career in soccer; that wasn't thought to be a stable enough career. Being in the armed services probably was more stable but when Veli wanted to follow through on his dream of becoming a pilot, via a career in the air force, Hareem refused to sign the paperwork. She had to be involved because he wasn't yet eighteen and she couldn't bear the thought of her only child potentially going to a war zone.

Veli became disillusioned and opted for an apprenticeship to be a telephone technician with the General Post Office (GPO). He was good with his hands and had an amazing memory where numbers were concerned so it was a reasonable compromise. For a while.

He had three best friends through school and once they were old enough, they went on a couple of overseas trips together to Portugal and Spain. This took his mind off another big event that was looming: a wedding. Not a union of love though but rather an arranged marriage to his cousin Filomena. Hareem planned this to keep future property inheritances in the family.

She was one of four children and as the older generations passed on, and property was divided equally, this sometimes meant that she would receive a quarter, an eighth or even one sixteenth of a building or block of land. Whilst grateful for this, it wasn't very practical so to help with the situation her older brother 'managed' things for her and parcels of property were swapped between the two of them to allow consolidation. This would be more useful should either of them ever want to sell, except that sometimes, unfortunately, her brother wasn't completely honest.

To minimise that happening with the next generation as well, Hareem thought that if the cousins married it would at least reduce dealings by one transaction! The only problem was they didn't love one another.

Veli's strict upbringing and the controlling nature of his mother, meant that the wedding was more of an ordeal than a celebration, so he didn't want his own friends to attend. And they didn't. The rest of the Turkish community did though: hundreds attended a big 'do' in Islington Town Hall.

The newlyweds took a floor of the big house and tried to make a go of it, but Veli wasn't happy. He went on holiday to Kos and had a chance meeting with an Albanian man who had extensive property interests in Australia which included a tobacco farm at Mareeba, in northern Queensland. Veli lamented his situation, so the man took pity on him and gifted him a flight to Australia to 'find himself'. He also gave him a job picking tobacco and in return Veli played for the local Albanian soccer team!

This was all good in principle, but the work didn't suit Veli: despite being a smoker himself, his arms had a reaction to the raw poison in the tobacco. He lasted three weeks. Not one to shy away from work, he took an unusual role as the 'off-sider' to a fluorspar prospector. This meant pacing out and measuring virgin bush land. The conditions were extreme even by Australian standards, but for the Cypriot boy who grew up in London, they were extraordinary. There was even a close encounter with a venomous taipan snake when he found himself between the snake and the skin it was shedding!

Thankfully Veli soon got news about a job that could use his telephone technician skills from the GPO and he moved even further north to the Comalco company-run town of Weipa. This obscure place on the west coast of Cape York, was the world's largest bauxite mine and is where our worlds would overlap, but not just yet. After six months away, it occurred to him that he might consider going back to London, but when he checked the details on the calendar, he'd missed returning to his old job by just one day, so figured he would stay and try to make the best of it.

Meanwhile in London, Filomena figured that if Veli was staying away they may as well divorce; so she organised the paperwork for him to sign. She sent it 'via Comalco' but unfortunately Veli didn't ever receive it. After more time, Filomena's father pressured her into following her husband Down Under (a popular nickname for Australia) which she did, and became pregnant a couple of years later.

This was the same man who didn't come home for forty days when Filomena herself was born! He was grieving having a daughter despite already having one son. She possibly spent her whole life trying to prove to him that she was as good as a second son would have been. By the way, he went on to have two more sons...

The Weipa Hospital wasn't suitable for childbirth so Zoe, Veli's daughter was born in the nearest large town which was actually five hundred miles away: Cairns. Filomena was supported by an older couple Bernie and Myrna who Zoe came to refer to as pseudo grandparents. Bernie and Veli were actually business partners. Bernie and Myrna used to live in Weipa also and owned the local cinema. When it was time for Bernie to retire, Veli bought into the business as an extra activity and they were partners for a few years until Veli owned it outright. It was run out of the town hall 'open space' and, when I went there, the 'village girl' was amused by the idea of watching a movie and having bats fly in front of the screen!

Zoe went to primary school in Weipa, Filomena got a worthwhile job and Veli found himself being the telephone technician, movie projectionist and very hands-on dad. After a few years though, Filomena decided that rather than having an 'Aussie' daughter who only knew English she wanted a Turkish one and the best way for this to happen was if she was going to school in Turkey!

Veli took long service leave and the family went on an extended trip to Turkey to find a school for Zoe. When the holiday time was up, Veli returned to Weipa to tidy up affairs and was then to go back to Turkey to maintain the family unit.

He decided instead though, that he was settled in Weipa, living as an Australian and didn't want to go back to his Turkish roots. In Weipa he moved from a family home to the Single Persons Quarters (SPQ).

4: From 'Concord' to 'The In Crowd' to Tropical Queensland

Fulmer Village School became Fulmer First School and when I was eight I had to progress to a 'middle' school in GX. I wasn't alone: a few friends went too, including Christine, Tony and Peter. I was still finding my confidence though and remember, for example, deciding to have cello lessons just because Christine did. Goodness knows what I was thinking… I didn't ever really enjoy it and persisted for several years including taking exams!

In the second year at GX Primary, I randomly became involved in a student swap to balance gender between two classes. Apparently they took the 6th, 12th and 18th girls in the roll and swapped them with boys by the same method. I hadn't really been friends with Rosemary and Jacqui previously and still wouldn't with Rosemary, but Jacqui and

I became 'besties'. We hung out together at school and then after school. She lived in GX in a huge house that was so interesting to me. They had lots of art on the walls and other fascinating things: I loved handling her Mum's carved stone eggs and there was an 'Oscar' in the downstairs loo. Yes, a *real* Academy Award!

Jacqui's dad Rob, was an art director in the movies. Some sets were made at Pinewood Studios and others required him to be away on location, sometimes for months at a time. Usually he went alone but sometimes, especially if the timing worked in with school holidays, the whole family would go.

Something about this family was to have a big impact on me in my adult life: they had parties. Often, or so it seemed. My family didn't have parties. Ever. Well except once for Maxie's 80th birthday. It made sense for Jacqui's family to have parties though. If Rob had been away for a few months, having a party was an easy way for him to catch up with everyone as soon as he returned home.

I yearned to be social. It wasn't that my parents didn't have *any* friends. They had friends in the motorcycle world, but they didn't come to our house. Ever. Well except once when William and Janet from Adelaide in Australia came for dinner. I didn't realise it at the time but that meeting would ultimately be a turning point in my life. Pa and William were both elected committee members for the Federation of International Motorcycling[xviii] which is the global body for all motorcycle racing.

As I progressed through school, Pa progressed through serving the motorcycle world. He was on multiple committees: some local, some national and some international. Some gave his family perks, such as when we went to the World Speedway Final at Wembley Stadium or other international events.

GX Primary gave me lots of happy memories but there were also some that weren't so flash. Around the time that Concorde made its first commercial flight, I was struggling with being called 'Concorde'! Some of the school kids thought that my nose made a striking resemblance to that amazing aircraft. Other times I was called 'four eyes' because I wore glasses. I felt sad and lonely around this bullying and was relieved when the school created roles for a couple of librarians. Jacqui and I were honoured to be asked and the really good part (read *sad* actually) was it meant we could stay inside in the library during breaks and I didn't have to go outside where the ridiculing was most intense.

It wasn't just the boys who teased me as some of this continued through to my girls-only high schools. When the movie Grease came out I had the nickname 'Eugene'. Some of the girls saw it many times and completely 'got into it' whereas this girl from The Village was lucky to get to the cinema for it, once. And when I did I realised 'Eugene' was the gullible, goofy, nerdy *guy*...

I had an unlikely ally at The Brudenell School in Brooke. We had met in the summer holidays before high school at a gymnastics club. Brooke took a shining to me and, quite frankly I was terrified of her. She seemed to be everything that I wasn't: confident, tall, pretty and an awesome swimmer. When she said she was going to the same school, I secretly hoped we wouldn't be in the same class but fate put us together, thankfully. We are still great friends today, even though we are as far apart globally as we could possibly be. Whilst I travelled to school on the bus from the village, our mothers would take it in turns to drive the nine miles to Amersham to collect us. On one of these occasions, I was persuaded to secretly carry a kitten home in my gym bag! No one would suspect me of doing something so naughty... Another friend Celia had a spare one and Brooke really wanted it. Of course once the cat was out of the bag, so to speak, it had found a new home.

There was a brush with fame at this school for a while in that Roald Dahl's youngest daughter Lucy joined us. I still treasure my author-signed copies of "Charlie and the Chocolate Factory" and "Charlie and the Great Glass Elevator".

Fame preceded me in the name of Sarah Brightman, the well-known singer and followed me in the name of Amal Clooney, who married the actor George Clooney, as fellow students attending Dr Challoner's High School. Whilst I excelled with my 'O Level'[12] results at Brudenell getting an almost 'clean sweep' of A's, when it really counted for entry to university I completely bombed-out as previously mentioned. My academic mind didn't cope well with the confusing relationship I had with my first boyfriend, who I refer to in the next chapter as Edward #1.

---

12   General Certificate of Education (GCE) Ordinary Level (O Level) is an exam taken at age sixteen in the UK.

This was the original Karma Chameleon 'disaster song' era. I had to re-group and re-do the year. For this I went to a college, almost in the shadows of Windsor Castle.

I was then ready to leave The Village and start over. I chose to do this in Bristol, a city exactly one hundred miles west. It straddled the River Avon and had a lots of elegant Victorian buildings, and a rich maritime history. It wasn't so far away though that I couldn't easily get back to The Village for the weekend sometimes or, as happened on a number of times, drive to London for music concerts. I recall two occasions when I drove to Wembley Stadium and back to Bristol again on the same night when Sir Elton John was playing! And, of course, another time to see Culture Club but they played at the more intimate Hammersmith Odeon.

Once I got to Bristol to study Business and Finance, I felt for the first time in my life that I was in the 'in crowd'. I was the 'land lady' for the student share house and could realise my dream of being more social! Whilst still carrying a bit of 'Miss Goody Two-Shoes', I enjoyed hosting parties and am still friends today with a few of those guests. One of them, John, lives less than an hour away from me at the Gold Coast, a popular tourist region near Brisbane, the capital of Queensland.

I can still recall the moment, lolling on a beanbag in my bedroom, when I decided that what I needed to do before embarking on adult life; was to backpack around Australia. I would contact William and Janet, start my tour in Adelaide and work for Comalco in Weipa. That may seem an unusual choice but twice during my studies, I did a six-month work placement at a lead and zinc smelter at Avonmouth, the industrial port near Bristol, which was also owned by CRA[13] which owned Comalco.

At that time, I was more than a little interested in owning a restaurant. I ended up at this smelter because they had recently installed a revolutionary catering system to feed their 24 hour workforce, and I had the opportunity to learn about that. Whilst there, I realised that they were planning on using the same system in Weipa and so I volunteered my services as I'd 'be there anyway'. This fact was sealed in a rather novel way by a chance encounter with Lord Shackleton[14] at a company fishing competition, of all things. My slightly increased confidence allowed me to strike up a conversation about my proposed adventure and he turned to my boss's boss's boss and said "You can organise this young lady a job in Weipa can't you?"

I had no idea at the time that no one is just *randomly* in Weipa. The employment contract was signed before I left The Village and as I started my working holiday backpacking adventure and telling people that I was working on the "west coast of Queensland" I began to get a feel for just how unusual that was. Most Australians would respond with "But Queensland doesn't have a west coast"!

And so it was. The girl from The Village ended up in a tropical, isolated town, populated mostly by single men and where every day killers were crocodiles, sharks and box jelly fish. She arrived during the storm that turned the dry season

---

13 Conzinc Riotinto of Australia Ltd (CRA).
14 Son of the Antarctic explorer and Vice Chairman of Rio Tinto Zinc Ltd (RTZ)

into the wet season. It was 38 degrees Celsius. She was wearing a hot pink track suit and the backpack containing all her worldly goods caught a different plane, leaving her in just what she was wearing!

By this time the man from the divided island had been there for fifteen years.

Veli and I both worked for the 'town office'. This was a small community, who supported the infrastructure of the town, all of which was owned by Comalco: including the houses, SPQ, power, water and feeding the single people. Ken was the Town Manager/quasi Mayor and I'm grateful that he made the decision to hire me for three months (which became five).

Ken's personal assistant Theresa was charged with my 'meet and greet'. Coincidentally her husband Tim, was the Air Queensland Manager and ran the airport. I couldn't have been in better hands for being 'luggage-less'. Rather than going straight to my special SPQ room which was actually SWQ (Single Women's Quarters – of which there were only six rooms next to the police station), we went via Theresa's house so she could loan me some clean undies, shorts and t-shirts. It was lucky we were a similar size! And luckily, I was re-united with my own clothes the next day. They had been sent to Bamaga, a small town which is even further north near the tip of Cape York.

On my first day at work, I was driven to my HR appointment by the most racist man I've ever met. He informed me that the Town Office Christmas party was the next weekend and

I was to avoid Veli at all costs citing "You can't trust these bloody Arabs!"

Theresa said Veli was all right and he seemed so. It certainly wasn't 'love at first sight' for me, although he later said it was so for him. We became friends and I was dragged along to 'dawn busters' golf for beginners on a Sunday morning, where we formed a friendship that was like brother and sister. I didn't feel the seventeen year age difference between us.

I liked that Veli seemed mature and 'happy go lucky' at the same time. He behaved as a single person and seemed to be involved in most of the multitude of sports available. These ranged from individual pursuits like tennis to team sports like cricket and volleyball. He was especially entrenched in the soccer community and was coach for many teams including eight groups of children at the nearby indigenous community of Weipa South.

As we became closer, we spent more time together, but didn't become lovers – although by now the town gossips were talking. Especially after one night when we chatted for hours in his SPQ room whilst drinking Galway Pipe port. I became tired and slept the night on his bed; he slept in the armchair. Veli dropped me back to the SWQ at about 5 a.m. the next day and a person who saw his car there reported that he had spent the night in my room! We were the hot topic of conversation at the communal breakfast.

This story was re-shared at the 'Chicken and Champagne Farewell Brunch' Theresa organised at her home, before we moved the party to the airport for my departure. Yes, drinks in eskies[15] and glasses were transported to the grass next to the tarmac at the airport... such a thing wouldn't happen in a city! Anyway, the laughing congregation joked that "and then he asked her to marry him". With that, a pretend engagement ring was crafted out of the metal cage from a champagne bottle cork. Then we posed for photos – me sitting on his lap. It was the first time we were physically so close.

I received 'royal' treatment on the plane and once settled, opened a handwritten letter from Veli. He had handed it to me as he left Theresa's, saying he was too upset to come to the airport. In the letter he said that he loved me and he wished there wasn't such an age difference between us.

---

15 Esky is an Australian brand of portable cooler and is now often used as a term to refer to coolers in general.

5: The Backpacker's Whirlwind Romance

I always knew I was going to live in Brisbane. I didn't know how or why but before I had even landed in Adelaide to start my Antipodean Adventure I 'had a feeling' about it.

After our brother-sister friendship in Weipa, the pace of my relationship with Veli picked up once I'd left Cape York. I had three goals that didn't include him: to do a PADI (Professional Association of Diving Instructors) diving course in Cairns, to be in Brisbane for the opening of World Expo '88 on 30th April *and* be back in The Village by Paula's 21st birthday and the parental's silver wedding anniversary in June.

Things started OK. The diving experience was fabulous, especially spending the night on the deck of a boat under the stars; we didn't do things like that in The Village!

The novelty of the diving wore off fairly quickly though, because I had trouble with my ears and ended up temporarily partially deaf, which was very scary.

I was staying with Danielle, the daughter of some friends from Weipa, and it was just before Easter. I noticed that a huge Easter egg appeared in the fridge but our paths didn't cross much and she failed to tell me until after Easter that it was actually for me! Veli had a few friends living in Cairns and he'd asked one of them – a school teacher called Zara – to purchase an egg and deliver it for me, from him.

It was actually my second gift from Veli whilst being in Cairns, that he had organised but not physically been involved in. The first was a friendship ring. At our last 'dawn busters' golf game in Weipa, he'd mentioned to me that we had such a special friendship he'd like it remembered with a ring. He had contacted Golightly's Jewellers in Cairns and I was to go there and choose something I liked. That felt special and weird at the same time. So there I was, the backpacker from The Village, selecting a ring for myself, from him. The only one I really liked that was suitable (and NOT obviously an engagement ring) was gold with seven tiny diamonds. The assistant was quite insistent "If that's the one you love then that is the one you should have - Mr Hassan was quite clear about that".

Back in 1988, we didn't have mobile phones and cheap international calls. Most weeks I'd go to the bank and get $100 in $1 coins to make phone calls from the telephone box. On this particular Sunday night, I was feeling very sick, lonely and scared about my deafness. I'd walked to the phone box down the road to call the parentals and they weren't home. So I called Veli. He was home. Or at least in his SPQ donga[16].

He queried whether I'd been to the doctor and I hadn't. He said he'd take me. I queried how that could happen. He said he'd go to work the next day, tell them "Urgent important business had come up in Cairns" (his business partner from the movie theatre did live there after all), and get a seat on the one flight of the day.

And so he did. Tuesday morning he arrived and took me to the doctor. I indeed had a serious ear infection that needed immediate medical intervention. It was lovely to feel looked after.

He'd booked a single room at Hydes Hotel. That meant it had two single beds. I guess he wasn't being presumptuous about what may happen. He was simply being my brother-friend and looking after me. There was something special about that though, and of course, by then I had read the letter on the plane.

One thing led to another and we spent the most idyllic four days in and around Cairns. We saw his friends Bernie and Myrna and heard stories of gold prospecting. We dined at Dukes, a popular restaurant, then sat around the grand piano sipping Galway Pipe port. We spent a day driving around the Atherton Tablelands and competed to see who could do the longest headstand. It was four days of bliss. Then Veli had to go back to work!

---

16   Single room accommodation.

And I went back to being a backpacker.

One thing I noticed about being a backpacker travelling solo is that I believe it led me to many more opportunities to be hosted by locals than if I had a companion. As I met new friends along the way they'd say "When you go to 'blah' you *must* stay with my parents/sister/friends/and so on". And I did. Often. It was, amongst other things interesting, delightful and inexpensive. And led to some lifelong friendships I still have thirty years on. Kerry and Johnny with the sugar cane farm at Ingham, a small township, 150 miles south of Cairns, fall into this category and of course, Nicole who introduced me to them. Nicole and I became friends because her (now deceased) husband Owen was a police officer and I would see police regularly when moving in or out of my SWQ room. Before Weipa Owen was stationed in Ingham.

Other friends I made for myself because, when you're alone, either you start talking to other 'solos' or they start speaking with you. Kevin and Cheryl fall into this category. We were in the 'Red Centre' in the geographical middle of Australia at an information session about the environment. It was a packed auditorium and I randomly sat next to Cheryl, who had her younger son Mitchell on her lap. When the educator mentioned quondongs (a wild bush fruit eaten by the local aboriginals), Mitchell said very loudly "Mum did he say condom?" Cheryl tried to quieten him down but he repeated it "Mum did he say condom?" And then "Mum – you've got wax in your ears." Cheryl was squirming and I just tried to ignore them and learn from the man on stage.

When the session was over, we got up and the crowd filed through the shop. Cheryl re-connected with Kevin, who had been standing at the back with their other son Robert. She simply said to me "So you liked my son's comments?" Obviously she'd noticed me smirking. I smiled politely and in the busy crowd, we didn't have a proper conversation.

That would happen just minutes later, when the universe put us as the only five people at the 'Watch the sun set behind the Olgas' (a nearby mountain range) viewing station.

We had a lovely hour together chatting and taking photos. I learned that they were from Sydney, the state capital of New South Wales. I was planning to visit Sydney just a few weeks later before heading to Weipa to work. As a couple they respected not being overt in front of me, but as soon as we parted ways, they had a quick chat with one another and then stopped me. By now it was completely dark. They invited me to stay with them in Sydney so I rummaged in my bag for my diary notebook and, in the shadows under the stars, Kevin wrote their phone number down.

I stayed with them for about three weeks in October – November 1987 before Weipa (when Kevin notoriously said "Watch out for all those blokes up there") and for a week in May 1988 before my return to the UK. During those few days, Kevin spoke with Veli on the phone and joked "Gees – if you were going to find a bloke up there, from all the thousands, couldn't you have picked an Aussie not a Pom?" He could hear the cockney still in Veli's voice as I could! Later, Kevin gave me away when I married Veli. We will be friends for life.

So many people were so kind to me that I live by a rule now that I call 'The Traveller's Bank of Love': those who make deposits are not necessarily those who make the withdrawals. It's an energy exchange around the universe. I certainly have hosted these mentioned friends and many others in my home. But I've also hosted friends of friends who I hadn't previously met because I valued that part of my travelling journey. Staying with strangers because a mutual friend suggested it, added so much to the richness of my adventure.

Once I left Cairns, I had a tight schedule to stick to, so that I could be at the opening of World Expo '88 in Brisbane on 30th April. Queen Elizabeth II would be there that day so I thought it would be cool for me to be there as well.

I would travel south (mostly via bus) staying at selected towns along the way, mostly in homes. Mackay was one of those places where the reputation that preceded me meant someone actually left a key to the front door under a pot plant. The generosity of this amazes me to this day. It is not something that would have happened in The Village.

It was the home of parents of a Weipa work colleague and it was a good job that they were away because it meant Veli could call the telephone land line and we could speak for hours. Literally, $1500 worth of phone time – even he was surprised when he received the bill - but that was so much more convenient than me being in a telephone box!

After our whirlwind, romantic four days in Cairns, our relationship deepened over phone conversations and Veli said he wanted to see me again before I flew home to The Village. So, he had more 'urgent important business' to do that required a few days off. This time in Brisbane. Only trouble was, the rest of the world, including The Queen, were also planning on being in Brisbane then and accommodation was extremely scarce. He could find individual nights at city hotels but not five nights in the same venue. The only place for that was the very basic Boondall Hotel Motel. So that's where our love was sealed. Not very salubrious, but it didn't matter!

I spent those five days questioning Veli about his past life as by then I realised that I had fallen for a man who appeared to be single for the five months up to that point, but actually wasn't!

He didn't ever not have an answer for a question. Sometimes I would say "Don't you have any questions for me?" His response was always the same "I only have one question for you and I'll ask that when the time is right". Instinct told me it was the marriage question but I didn't dwell on it.

So, on the morning after I returned to The Village he telephoned and asked that question. After being lovers for exactly nine days, I said "Yes!"

If my son, or a special friend, or anyone for that matter, said they were getting married on the basis of a friendship of a few months and a bit of romance for four days, then five days with a few hours of phone conversation in between, I'd say they were mad. Or at least politely suggest they give it a bit more time. Love doesn't work that way though. I was determined and wouldn't have had anyone stand in my way.

Veli had actually rung the night before, when we had been home from the airport literally a few minutes. It was unlike him, but he'd mis-calculated the time and thought I'd been home for hours without letting him know. What had happened was the parentals, Paula and her then boyfriend Jim were all settling in the lounge to hear some stories about my travels and it would have been really rude for me to be distracted by talking on the phone. Especially as Edward #2 was there too. Poor Edward #2!

Prior to Veli I had two relationships with Edward #1 and Edward #2. They were great friends. There was actually another Edward too. I was never close to Edward #3 and didn't particularly like him, so much so, that even though he was backpacking Down Under at exactly the same time as me, I deliberately didn't plan to meet him. I simply said "If we're meant to meet we'll do it somewhere significant such as crossing the Sydney Harbour Bridge or at Ayers Rock". And of course the universe provided. We took one photo at the Yulara Resort near the famous Uluru (the official name of Ayers Rock was changed in December 1993) to prove that the unbelievable really did happen and then went our separate ways!

During school I struggled with feeling 'unpretty' and left out when my friends started to have boyfriends: I think I still felt tormented by the teasing about my glasses. Prior to my friend 'Aunty Sue' (who was actually my first real employer, if you disregard collecting eggs at the village farm) organising a blind date with Edward #1 for her own amusement because she thought we looked similar, my only other romantic encounter was being kissed by a boy in the German village of Konz-Oberemmel when I was an exchange student. Of course, his name was Eduard as well! It was just spelt slightly differently.

So English Edward #1 lasted a couple of years until he ditched me (remember the Karma Chameleon 'disaster song') to return to his previous beau Karina who happened to be Edward #3's sister. If social media is to be believed, it looks like they are still together now.

He was a coward though and didn't even tell me himself. He sent Edward #2 as the messenger! The only thing was, Edward #2 had secretly been admiring me for that same couple of years. And we'd spent a lot of time with one another. There were many times when the three of us had hung out together including at Edward #2's parent's house and weekends at a farm in Kent which Edward #1 owned with his two brothers.

Edward #2 was one of the loveliest young men on the planet. The only thing was I didn't love him. I thought I might grow to though because he was so 'nice'. Eventually I gave in to his advances to try. This was during my time in the student share house. He drove the hundred miles to visit me quite often and the relationship was pleasant enough but not 'right'.

Once I decided to go backpacking – perhaps creating some excitement for myself, that wasn't in our very stable relationship – I tried to break up with him. I suggested he didn't wait for me and that we see how we felt on my return, which was originally to be six months. He gave me a gold St Christopher pendant to stay safe and I wore it dutifully. Despite having a small chain, I also wore a tiny coral tulip that the parentals gave me as a gift from Japan and along the way a gold kangaroo was added as a souvenir.

After nine months, I returned and Edward #2 had contacted the parentals about being part of the welcoming committee at the airport. They had no reason to think anything other than that this was a good thing. When I came through the gates looking, although I say so myself, radiant and tanned and wearing a Snowy River[xix] Akubra[17] hat, my heart sank as soon as I saw him. It wasn't his fault, it was the new me.

There were three cars at the airport, including that of Edward #2 and the parentals had already invited him home to The Village so I was obliged to travel with him. It was a very difficult half an hour and he wanted to make plans. I said I was very tired and would call him the next day.

After a bit of socialising with drinks and food, Edward #2 and Jim left. I had a shower then remember lolling on Paula's bed and telling her about Veli. I had a couple of photos of us in Cairns that I shared and her first comment was "Ooh you'll have lovely coloured children". He had olive skin that was darkened by sixteen years of Weipa sun.

---

17   Akubra is an Australian company that traditionally makes wide-brimmed bush hats out of rabbit felt.

6: The Man in the Village

The next morning as soon as I woke up, the phone rang and it was Veli. He asked me "How's that one percent going?" When I replied "What one percent?" he asked me to marry him. Just like that. I hadn't even been back in The Village twelve hours.

The significance of the question was not lost on me, although it was a bit obscure. When I spent those five days in Brisbane questioning Veli and he'd said he only had one question for me, we had discussed that I was ninety-nine percent sure what my response would be. As soon as I saw

Edward #2 at the airport, I knew I could never marry him. I also knew that the concept of marrying Veli was actually completely mad, but I wanted to give it a go because if I didn't try I would never know and may regret it for the rest of my life. He was seventeen years older than me, from a completely different culture, living in a remote place on the other side of the world, had a twelve year old daughter and was actually technically still married to someone else. Wow! But get married we did. Twice.

After popping the question to me, he asked if Pa was home. However he had already gone to work. So Veli spoke with Ma and asked her for my hand in marriage. She cried. Veli also asked for Pa's work phone number and thank goodness didn't get through to him. Understandably, the questions flowed and the parentals were concerned.

Until this point I had a reputation for being 'The Sensible One'. The sensible daughter. The sensible employee: despite my young age, 'Aunty Sue' had left her business in my youthful hands on a few occasions whilst she went on overseas holidays. The sensible landlady in the student share house. How could such hectic madness be happening to me?

I rang Edward #2 and arranged to visit him in the afternoon. I didn't 'beat about the bush' but came straight out with my news – I'd met someone on my travels and was going to migrate to Brisbane! I didn't stay long. Apparently he had a bottle of Moet & Chandon champagne in the fridge and was all ready to toast 'us' and my safe return. Apparently he threw the bottle out of the window and it made a big mess. I didn't ever mean to hurt him and was sorry that he was so devastated.

Migrating to Australia to get married was extraordinarily quick for me. There was a major detail in that Veli needed to get divorced but he thought that would be seamless because Filomena and he had already been separated for more than a year. Only trouble was, she was still waiting for him to return, and so was his daughter Zoe. With hindsight, it probably would have been better if Veli had gone to share his news in person, rather than over the phone.

Veli was also challenged managing everything from Australia; time differences and working meant he struggled with some of the administration. His initial attempt at finding a copy of his first marriage certificate failed dismally and momentarily he joked that perhaps he wasn't even properly married to Filomena. It was a bit ironic that it was my dealings with Islington Town Hall, which led to a copy of the appropriate document.

He filed for divorce and Filomena rebelled the whole way. He arranged a wedding date for us by looking up names of celebrants in the Yellow Pages, as part of my paperwork required a statement from a marriage celebrant that a booking had been made. I would travel on a 'fiancé visa' which meant I could be deported if we didn't get married three months after my return to Australia. It was so handy that from The Village I could easily travel to Australia House in London and physically drop off documents, as they became available to me. This included things like a full medical with chest x rays.

One of Pa's stipulations was that Veli should come to The Village as soon as possible to meet everyone. We knew this was important but other factors that affected timing included the progress of my visa application, the progress of Veli's divorce and how much time he could take off work. We wanted all these dates to align. Which of course they did, but there was some intense nurturing along the way to make it happen.

Veli arrived in The Village early on a Friday morning in August 1988. After a few hours of 'getting to know one another' he and I went to Windsor shopping. Windsor where the castle is. There were a couple of 'big ticket' items on the shopping list. My friend's Vanessa and Vince were getting married the next day and Veli needed to wear a suit, and I needed an engagement ring to complement my friendship ring. Veli had asked me to have a think about what I'd like and I'd seen one in the window of a shop in Windsor. I hadn't tried it on though. That was the reason for going to Windsor over any of the other local towns.

That night we went for dinner with the parentals, Paula and Jim. Veli presented me with the ring and then surprised me with a Cartier watch. He had a Cartier that I absolutely loved but the one he bought me was completely different and had a brown leather strap. We didn't know one another well enough for Veli to know that brown was my worst colour. However, I was grateful and still wore it with pride. Later on, after enough years had passed, I thought I could reasonably get away with it and changed the strap.

It was lovely going to a wedding and in fact the reception was at the Burnham Beeches Hotel where we would later have our (second) wedding reception.

The following weekend I had another wedding in my diary but I would go to this one alone. I was to be a bridesmaid for Brooke in Greenwich. Not the one an hour away but the one an hour from New York. So, after the intense build-up to Veli's arrival, the following weekend, I would leave him alone with my parents! Not ideal, but with so many other things going on, it wasn't the right time for us to have a romantic trip to a wedding in the USA. It was commonplace from the 1980's onwards for some people to spend the weekend in The Big Apple from London. So that's what I did. Completely mad perhaps but 'hectic' was my middle name in that era. It didn't seem so at the time though. I was just following the bouncing ball and ticking things off the list. Best friend's wedding. Tick. Another best friend's wedding – Oh that one's in America, sort it out. Tick. My wedding – Oh that one's in Australia, sort it out. Tick.

So, sort it out we did.

Surreptitiously.

7: A Wedding, Times Two

The parentals decided they wouldn't make our wedding be the reason for their first trip Down Under. We were under time pressures imposed by the government and they already had another overseas trip booked and paid for (to Rio de Janeiro) because of Pa's service to worldwide motorcycle sports. If they couldn't be at our wedding, they didn't want to know the details including the date. They didn't want to be fretting about not being with us. And so it was, and I understood.

The plan (for them) was that we would get married in secret and let them know afterwards. We would have a second ceremony the next year in The Village that was really all about them, and we did.

I'm still moved to tears when I think about the parentals crying at the airport when we left. We travelled back to Brisbane via Singapore where I would get a fabulous wedding gown made. The year before on my way to Adelaide I had spent a week in Singapore and there was a bridal shop in the arcade under the hotel I stayed at. I didn't have a serious look back then as I didn't have a serious need but I'd established enough to know that it would be quite an economical plan. Veli and I allowed a week so I could be measured up and then have the frock stitched to perfection.

When I went to the shop, there was one that I loved that fitted me perfectly. Of course there was! I questioned then, why I would get another one made just for the sake of it? We made the purchase the next day and changed our flights. We didn't need to be hanging around Singapore just for the sake of it... we had a home to set up. And quickly because Veli had to get back to Weipa to work. Exciting times ahead.

Veli owned an apartment on the river in Toowong in Brisbane. It was rented out but the timing worked so the tenants moved out and Veli had it re-painted for us. A blank canvas for a new life together.

After a few days he went back north and would apply for jobs in Brisbane from there. I would organise our home and look for work myself. He was successful in getting interviews for the first few jobs he applied for and realised he couldn't do the process justice from 1,500 miles away. So he flew back to Brisbane, went to the interviews, got all the jobs, chose the one that appealed most, then flew back to Weipa to resign! He'd arrived at Weipa with a suitcase, sixteen years before, and left with a suitcase. In between he'd had a daughter, 'lost' a wife and family, and found love for the first time.

Despite initiating her return to Turkey with their daughter, Filomena wasn't going to give up their marriage without a fight. They had worked hard between their Comalco jobs and the cinema to capitalise on their inheritances and owned a few properties in Kos, Turkey and the one apartment in Brisbane. Despite a huge imbalance in value, Veli was prepared to walk away from the overseas property portfolio and just keep a roof for us.

Filomena denied receiving the divorce documents, despite referring to them in other legal correspondence. It was a tense time for us and Veli actually had to fly to Townsville for the divorce, with a barrister in tow. There was a lot riding on it: time was running out on my fiancé visa and we needed the divorce date plus a month before we could follow through on our wedding plans. We made it with four days to spare.

As the timing was close, Veli joked about getting married on my birthday. I said no to this as I didn't want the celebration flowers or other gifts combined every year! A few decades later I would come to realise the significance of this decision and be grateful for it.

So we were married the day after my birthday. A Sunday afternoon on the riverbank – downstairs from the apartment we made home. We didn't know many people, so the guest list was small. Nicole and Owen from Weipa, Zara from Cairns (who'd purchased the Easter egg for me), my primary school friend Fiona and her friend Kayla – because they were backpacking and 'just passing through', and Kevin and Cheryl from Sydney. Absent were Margaret and Thomas who would become our 'Christmas Family' and who had chosen that exact weekend to visit Sydney for the first time in years.

I didn't wear the 'meringue gown' from Singapore but instead I wore a Flora Kung of New York. It was a huge shoulder padded, brightly coloured, floral frock and has been worn many times since for dress-up parties. It *was* still the 1980's! I had a white silk straw hat, lace gloves and stiletto sling-back sandals. I really looked dressed for the races and struggled with the hat in the wind. We had champagne, telephoned the parentals to share our news, then went in a couple of taxis to the city for a paddle wheeler river cruise; where we ate seafood on the Kookaburra Queen.

Eight months later, rather than just seven guests, we had the more conventional 'do' in The Village. This was really for my family as Veli, still didn't have anyone he wanted to celebrate with, except for a couple of school friends (one of whom came but the other was on holiday and couldn't.). He'd had a falling out with his parents, who were living between their house at Highbury in London and a small farm in Kos.

Apparently during a previous disagreement between Filomena and Hareem, Filomena gave Veli an ultimatum to choose between his wife and his mother! For the sake of his daughter Zoe, he chose Filomena and then didn't speak with his parents for sixteen years. I tried to pave the way for a reconciliation and by the time my sister Paula was married a number of years later (to Robin not Jim!) they were 'back in the fold' and invited.

When we had the appointment with the rector about the church service, there was a scary moment when we thought Veli's Muslim birth had caused a problem, even though he'd never actually been in a mosque and didn't own a copy of the Quran. It turned out though that the priest really was concerned because he'd been married before. Instead of having a 'Blessing' for our marriage we had to use another convoluted name for the event: it was a 'Service of Prayer and Dedication'.

Despite booking a chauffeur and vintage Rolls Royce, Veli and I walked from the parentals' house down the lane to the church with our bridesmaids Paula and Brooke. The 'Roller' followed at a snail's pace behind us. We kept a hundred guests waiting when it got lost and then 'failed to proceed!' (they don't break down apparently!) on our way to the reception. Once finally there we had 'Pimms' on the lawn, followed by a lovely dinner and dancing.

The evening did end very sadly though. It was the era of newspapers and first editions being printed and delivered in the very early hours of the morning. Our party had ended but we were sitting around near the hotel reception and relaxing with a few close friends. As the papers arrived, news filtered through that whilst we had been celebrating, other people merrymaking on a boat called 'The Marchioness' on the River Thames in London had drowned when it hit a dredger[xx]. It's still London's worst river disaster. Fifty-one souls were lost and we have remembered them as part of our anniversary toasts every year.

A couple of weeks after our village celebration, we were back Down Under. Eventually. Our flights were delayed due to a pilot's Industrial Dispute[xxi]. We finally arrived home at 2 a.m., where there was a stack of mail. Whilst it wasn't all opened, there were three envelopes of particular interest because they bore the logo of our solicitor.

Not content with taking ownership of property in Kos and Turkey, Filomena was staking rights to a large percentage of our home. Despite one of the reasons Veli was surrendering property overseas (without making a claim) was so the rental income could fund Zoe's private schooling in Turkey. It seemed however, that Zoe was being brought to live with us!

One letter we opened said Filomena and Zoe were probably coming. The next one said they were definitely on their way. And a third one said they had arrived. And, *where were we*?

Mehtap, a distant cousin, was also living in Brisbane and we guessed that Filomena and Zoe would probably be with her family. We didn't sleep and waited till 7 a.m. to call them and find out.

At 9 a.m. the doorbell went. We 'buzzed' to open the main door downstairs. We lived on the third floor. When I opened our apartment door, there was an innocent girl with a suitcase. Zoe had been dropped off and was now alone. It transpired that Filomena had purchased a return ticket for herself and a one way ticket for Zoe.

I was twenty-four and had 'given birth' to a twelve year old. Life would never be the same again.

8: "*You* will make or break this family"

"*You* will make or break this family." They were strong words from my GP Dr Betty and they would define the next eight years of my life. She was an older English lady and in business with her husband Dr Vaughan. I generally saw her and Veli generally saw him. I respected her and so took on board her 'wise' words. She said as the 'mother', I had it in my power to make us a family that worked. Or not. Wow! What a huge responsibility. I didn't take it lightly and wasn't in the practice of not giving anything my best shot.

I knew from the beginning of course, that Veli had a daughter, but in my wildest dreams I didn't imagine that she would become 'my' daughter as well, especially so quickly and without any discussion. We will never know the real reasons why but the sort of things that crossed our minds included that she was a 'plant' to disrupt and ultimately destroy our marriage. We also heard that she was desperately unhappy living in Turkey - after all she was an Aussie kid - and just wanted to live Down Under. In fact early in 1989 Zoe had actually requested coming to live with us and I had arranged everything. When Veli called to give her the flight information, Filomena denied him access to speak with her. Supposedly Zoe had changed her mind. So we had moved on.

There were though, apparently, two suicide attempts and if there was a third then the Turkish authorities would remove her from Filomena's care. Filomena had some mental health issues as well and there was even talk of both of them sharing medication to overdose and jump out of a window together. Serious stuff!

Zoe was nervous, scared and bold all at the same time. Veli and I were happy living in the apartment and planned to do so until we had a baby of our own but having Zoe there was really like living with a third adult; the place wasn't large enough for that. Within days Zoe made comments like she hoped I would leave Veli for a younger man or, if I had a baby she'd be 'very interested' in Veli's reaction to it. She had hatred in her tone of voice to Veli which worried me and my motherly instinct told me to not only mediate and try to calm the situation but also that I didn't want to have a baby whilst she was around.

An early drama that highlighted our cultural differences was an incident with wax. In The Village in the 1970s when I transitioned into womanhood, we used shavers or depilatory creams. In the Middle East they use wax and obviously start young. I can't even recall how Zoe came to have the wax but I assume she purchased it with her own money and started dealing with it one day when I was out. I came home to find wax drips all over the bathroom! I was not happy. I think there were a couple of things going on in my mind including that I had only just started waxing myself (but paying someone else to do it for me) and now here was my daughter doing it too. But not with the competence to keep her surroundings clean.

From day one we dined at the table. The dining room table. Together, because that's what we did in The Village and I didn't know any other way. It wasn't planned because I was doing what came naturally to me as a family-maker, but to Zoe sitting at the table to eat would be a first and, unbeknown to me initially, perhaps one of the most appreciated aspects of my parenting. She mentioned from time to time that, whilst her mother had a dining suite, and a marble one at that, it was for 'show' rather than actually being used! I was flabbergasted but the emotion with which Zoe shared the story led me to believe it to be true.

Whilst in Turkey, Zoe had attended a private boarding school; in Brisbane she went to the local government run establishment. She settled in quite well and was quite bright. When, after a year, we finally moved to a large house on the other side of town, she elected to still go to that original school. The distance was a nuisance though and bus travel added hours to the school day. I sensed that Zoe was gravely unhappy and felt she had no friends. She wouldn't admit too much but there was a day when I sensed a suicide attempt may be on the cards.

I've always been good with intuition but on this occasion I think my newly found motherly instinct or super strong sixth sense kicked in. I felt compelled to remove and hide most of the tablets from the family medicine box. I didn't want this to be too obvious though so left some there.

I was working for a Brisbane-based information technology (IT) company. What started as two days of temporary administration work, doing some photocopying and binding became a fourteen year career in a variety of roles. One of those was as personal assistant to the general manager and I can still recall the day I answered my phone to hear Zoe say "I've overdosed on Panadol[18] but don't worry I've called the Kid's Helpline[19] [xxii] and they've called an ambulance for me". Wow!!!

Was it my sixth sense or mother's instinct? Perhaps she wouldn't be alive today if I hadn't removed most of the medication. I wonder what or even if she'd have done anything else instead if I had removed all of it? We will never know.

I rang Veli and we met at the Emergency Department. It seemed like my worst nightmare and I was completely out of my depth with mothering now. In my mind she needed to see a psychiatrist or psychologist and perhaps take some prescription medication. After a few days in hospital it was me who went from clinic to clinic trying to find someone

---

[18] Panadol is a brand of paracetamol for mild pain relief which is easily available in supermarkets and pharmacies.

[19] Kid's Helpline is a confidential phone counselling service for young people aged 5-25 years.

who she would 'gel' with and want to talk through what was going on. I was playing out what I thought any mother would do and she seemed to be playing out being obstinate, difficult and rebellious.

After her hospital visit, Zoe didn't want to go back to the original school and half way through grade twelve – the final year of high school – she transferred to a school close to where we lived.

All this time she only had intermittent contact with her mother: nothing for months and then she'd receive a 'lovey-dovey' card full of hundreds of dollars in cash.

By the time of the second overdose – and, of course, one of the ambulance guys was the same. "Gees I think I've been to this house before" apparently came out of his mouth on arrival – I was completely 'over' the whole thing, especially as it revolved around a demand for her former boyfriend Aaron to take her back after dropping her. I was with her as she vomited in the Emergency Department. My clothes got splattered black from the charcoal formula she'd been given to heal her stomach and expel the drugs. I can remember being angry rather than sympathetic. That isn't how I'd feel now but back then that's how it was. I was so young myself. And terrified!

There were just thin curtains between us and other medical emergencies. I couldn't help but be aware of the old man in the next cubicle who'd just had a heart attack and the scared emotions of his loved ones. Then there was the screaming boy who'd broken his leg in a remarkable accident at school sports. These other people seemed deserving of their beds and us being there seemed avoidable somehow. After all, I had been traipsing around town with Zoe trying to get help for her for months.

I was exhausted and scared. At my 'wits end'. Thank goodness for the advice of my work colleague Esther... something that, nearly thirty years on, I am reminded of and repeat to others. She wisely said to me "Well if Zoe won't get help or can't find a suitable psychiatrist, then get one for yourself". Wow. It had never occurred to me before. I didn't seem like the sick one – although if I were to be really honest, mental health issues have probably been around for at least as far back as the 'Karma Chameleon' era.

The idea was like a 'breath of fresh air'. It immediately resonated with me and, of course, being the person that I am, I acted straight away.

Another friend had a few issues and used to see someone they referred to as 'The Witch'. Whilst this doesn't sound like a great starting point, I was assured that 'The Witch' was a great practitioner (a psychologist at the Wesley Hospital) and there would be value in her tough love and straight talking.

So I started seeing 'The Witch'. Then I persuaded Veli to come along too because, even though I've only been talking about me, of course he was scared and angry and at the end of his tether as well. He was ready to 'wipe' Zoe and send her back to her mother. Whilst I was on a path of "Being the glue to keep the family together" à la Dr Betty, he was over it and wanted us to go back to being just us. He also had a financial reason for wanting this.

Veli had voluntarily given up all his overseas property assets to provide for Zoe's education and now here we were bringing her up. Not only that, he had fought to even keep the apartment we used to live in and had 'wasted' tens of thousands of dollars on legal fees to do so.

Sessions with 'The Witch' weren't pleasant but they were certainly useful. In fact, one of the concepts she talked about in relation to two or more people recalling exactly the same event completely differently, would become part of my 'bag of tricks' two decades later.

On the second suicide attempt, after spending hours at the hospital, we went home for much needed sleep only to be woken at 1.30 a.m. with a call from the hospital to say Zoe had been discharged and would we collect her? Of course, we obliged to do so but then a surreal thing happened. She behaved completely normally – like we were perhaps just collecting her from a standard school day! She then requested that we drive from the hospital, just across the road to The Courier Mail newspaper headquarters, to buy a paper because it was the night the university entrance results were published. We found out she was admitted to the University of Queensland to study Science. The only trouble was that her subject selection was to please her mother rather than herself, so she only lasted a few months!

Through this time, whilst I worked in IT, we also ran an electrical business. Just before I'd met Veli he'd correctly predicted the change in telecommunications technology and become an electrician as an adult apprentice. Despite competing with teenagers in Weipa, he'd fought for a place and excelled. After a year or so in his initial job in Brisbane, he quit to "do his own thing". So, after spending my whole childhood in The Village living in a home that ran a small business, I was doing so again.

I really enjoyed the initial process of organising logos and other branding for the stationery, vehicle and so on. As time progressed I found myself with the extra job of entering invoicing data into the computer as I could and it wasn't really Veli's area of expertise.

Veli was good at talking to people to create work for himself and we soon discussed having team members and extra vehicles. In the end though he decided he didn't want to do that and was happier just having a job for himself. We had many contacts and one of these gave Zoe a job.

She worked as a shop assistant in the haberdashery department for David Jones, a large department store. This was never going to be a long-term career choice for such a bright girl, but it could have led to management training if she'd wanted that and applied herself. She didn't.

In the meantime, though, she thought she'd move out to a share house closer to work. Of course, we supported this by helping her move her bed, buying some electrical equipment and I even acquired some furniture during a work office move.

Zoe couldn't cope with life on her own though and after a few months she pleaded to be able to return to our home. We duly obliged, then she applied for university again. This time to Queensland University of Technology (QUT) to study International Marketing. She was still tending towards subjects to please her mother rather than to become a teacher which she really wanted.

Whilst we struggled with the teenage years in our house and I did my absolute best to hold the family together, it was remarkable that I had three friends who similarly found themselves mothering daughters who were abandoned by their birth mothers. It's more prevalent today than thirty years ago but still not an everyday occurrence; for it to be happening to me and three others in my close circle, gave me support from a different angle.

When Rae, Wendy, Beverley and I 'compared notes', even though they didn't have the extremes such as cultural differences and suicide attempts to deal with, they also had it tough. To be completely fair and acknowledge Veli, whilst I think he struggled with parenting, he did try to protect our relationship by putting me ahead of Zoe most of the time. He maintained the view that she was sent to destroy our marriage and he tried his hardest not to allow that to happen. Some of my friends struggled, because their partners put their daughters ahead of them. I was very grateful Veli didn't do this. Perhaps I put in an extra effort with Zoe to make up for this. I don't know: it certainly wasn't conscious.

I was continually frustrated with Veli's apparent inability to 'parent' Zoe, although I sense he was probably OK in

Weipa for the first few years of her life when he possibly spent more time with her than Filomena did. I often wonder what changed but have never thought to actually ask as I don't think he'd know, or believe there was anything actually 'wrong'.

A low-light of his parenting was when Zoe refused to get in the car when he went to collect her from the local skating rink. It was 11 p.m. and she told him to "F*** off". He never forgave her lack of respect for him.

Even though I was feeling my way at parenting a teenager, who I didn't even give birth to, no one will deny that I tried my absolute best: I couldn't have tried any harder if she'd come through my own loins. People knew that but the most important person to feel it was Zoe herself. In fact I think it bothered her deeply that, according to fable, step mothers are supposed to be wicked, and I wasn't. Worse than that, I wasn't even 'just all right', I was actually really nice and loving towards her! I believe she was torn because by being nice back she was worried that she was being disloyal to her own mother.

The irony in all this is that, despite my best efforts and trying to get professional help for her, Zoe was still mentally unstable. The suicide attempts and generally erratic behaviour led me to believe that I couldn't trust her if I had my own baby, so I put it off, for a whole eight years. We had a couple of friends from the Weipa days who had known her then, and also knew Filomena and they agreed with me.

And so it was. But not until Veli turned fifty. Zoe had gone back to Turkey for ten days before starting at QUT and stayed away for three years! I finally decided that my biological clock was ticking. It was time for me to have my baby. So I did.

9: Incompetent Mother

By the time we celebrated Veli's fiftieth birthday with a super fun wig party, I was wondering why I wasn't pregnant yet. My role at the IT company had developed into what I would find to be completely stimulating and made me feel valued: I flew around Australia training small teams in call centres to use a case management database system.

A couple of months later the magic did happen though and I found myself pregnant.

When I migrated to Australia and knew only a handful of people, I went out of my way to befriend people I met and who I liked. Randomly to that point, most of those new friends were older than me. In fact, they were closer in age to Veli than me which was fine and they doted on me as I blossomed out of shape. I decided that once I had my baby, I'd find some friends closer to my own age.

Kristina was the first of those. As we checked in for the pregnancy physio exercise class at the Wesley Hospital, we had to write our name and suburb on the list. As soon as I noticed Kristina lived five minutes away I made an extra effort to get to know her. Dana was next – she was the most fun at the ante natal classes and it didn't matter that she lived on the other side of town – I made a point of getting to know her too.

Then there was Donna. She too lived close, we met at the physio and our boys shared a birthday. In fact they would go on to share many birthdays as they went to kindy, then high school and university together. They skipped the togetherness of primary school but we all stayed friends anyway.

Even though it was nearly twenty years ago, I can remember a particular hospital moment like it happened today. One minute that changed my (mental) world. If it had really happened today I probably would have let it go because I now realise that me holding on to it is a choice, but I didn't have the capacity or 'mental management skills' for that back then.

It was about 2 a.m. on about day seven, of an eight day stay at the Wesley Hospital. I had been labelled as having the 'Baby Blues'[20]; very emotional and weeping often so, even though I'm typically quite social, the doctor prescribed no visitors by a sign on the door. As an aside, Veli had hardly

---

20 Mood swings and crying for no apparent reason in the few days immediately after having a baby.

spent any time with me in hospital because his only Turkish friend in Brisbane was doing a restaurant re-fit between Christmas and New Year and he 'had' to be there, supporting him during the day.

I had been struggling with feeding our new son, whom we called Ali, and he had finally gone to sleep. I may even have looked like I was asleep myself and didn't want to be disturbed when a different nurse walked in. Without even glancing at me she grabbed the clipboard, wrote something and left.

I was intrigued with what she had written as she hadn't taken any 'observations'; pulse and so on. And as I said, she hadn't even looked at me. It wasn't worth struggling out of bed for just that - my Caesarean section scar was still very painful - but I decided I'd be nosey next time I went to the bathroom.

A little while later when I reviewed the report it said 'Incompetent Mother'. INCOMPETENT MOTHER!!!

What on earth made her come to that conclusion? I'd never seen her before and we didn't engage in any way. In fact, if she looked at me or got close enough she would have known that I was awake. Did this mean I was a failure and the object of gossip amongst the nurses? If so, even "Would benefit from more support" would have been more helpful. To be honest, I probably would have agreed and been grateful for that. But no. Incompetent Mother!

There were many disappointing aspects to my stay at the 'Milton Hilton'[21]. It started well enough – a middle of the night emergency Caesarean section when my waters broke at midnight on Boxing Day. Ali was due on 12th January but was a very tight breach and we had been scheduled a delivery date of 6th January. Christmas Day was extremely hot and a few older and more experienced ladies amongst my 'Christmas Family' said I looked like I was about to burst and the baby wouldn't wait till the next year. After lunch I even went for a lie down for a couple of hours on the host's bed, under the fan.

Boxing Day was hotter again and I spent the whole day flopped over a beanbag in another friend's swimming pool to try and keep cool. Again a few people said I was about to 'pop!'

And so that night I did. Pop! I went to bed at 10.30 p.m. and Veli decided to watch a James Bond movie. Just after midnight, I wet the bed! Seriously. The floodgates had opened and I rushed to the shower. Even though it hadn't happened before and certainly wasn't in my plan, I figured out what was going on and thought to myself "If I'm going to hospital now, I don't know when my next shower will be so I may as well have a nice shower, then blow dry my hair!" We learned at antenatal classes that once the waters break you should deliver the baby within 24 hours as the sterile environment bubble has been burst. I figured a few more minutes to make me feel good was important.

---

21   A 'Jo-ism' for The Wesley Hospital.

I'd rung the hospital to let them know and by the time we arrived at about 2 a.m. a surgical team of seven was swiftly assembled. Some had been woken from sleep in their beds and rushed to support me. I couldn't fault this process. Ali was born ninety minutes later and life would never be the same again.

Once I got to my room though, things started to be not so systemised. At 7 a.m. we were disturbed by carpet cleaners with one of those huge, noisy machines. My catheter had overflowed and there was a flood on the carpet. How does that happen in this day and age, if it's being monitored regularly?

Anyway… a few other hospital memories include a cold shower. A *cold shower* at the Milton Hilton. So I guess there can randomly be a problem with the hot water any time. My issue was, as I was standing there naked with a screaming baby, a couple of metres away, I wasn't sure if I was even going mad and had the tap in the wrong position! When I hit the "Call Nurse" button, it took what seemed like forever for the nurse to arrive. She confirmed that there wasn't any hot water and so I had a cold shower. Not very comforting when I was so in need of nurturing. So then I changed rooms.

A delightful memory was the amount of flowers I received. Everyone that came to visit said my room looked like a florist. That's wonderful but they don't last forever. Normally they have special volunteers who have a role to look after flowers. A lovely idea but, because it was between Christmas and New Year, most of them were away. So my flowers, that were so pretty when they were fresh, started dying en masse and dealing with that was not of much interest to anyone other than me! It's such a silly thing in hindsight but the drama of getting rid of dead flowers is a sad hospital memory.

After eight days in hospital I took Ali home. Veli was still working crazy hours including at the Turkish restaurant. I didn't have any other support and the perfectionist in me wanted everything to be 'just right'. A healthy, calm baby, a tidy home, thank you cards written and posted and, to be HAPPY. After all… I had been waiting a decade for this moment.

I was so far from happy. I was completely exhausted and, I was waiting with trepidation for Zoe's return!

She had unexpectedly contacted me on Mother's Day in 1997 and was thrilled I was pregnant saying "I won't be an only child any more". She then emailed me regularly: sometimes daily and sometimes weekly. Despite her erratic behaviour she had mentioned a number of times she'd like a sibling, especially a brother: once she even gave me a baby name book. Of course I didn't ever let on that I was avoiding pregnancy around her, and when I heard her saying to her father Veli that she wanted to "Drink her grandmother's (Hareem's) blood" I felt vindicated in my decision.

A few months later she said, after considering options in the USA and UK, she'd like to come back to Australia to study and "Start over". I had organised a copy of her birth certificate so she could get an Australian passport, and course possibilities as it was very close to the application closing date. I couldn't believe it but felt compelled to 'go with the flow'. I didn't have the energy or heart to disagree. I would have to make it work as I had previously.

When Ali was exactly a month old, we all went to the airport to collect her and Zoe was only interested in her baby brother. I tried not to show it but I was terrified of her return and how our new family unit would get along. I now had a baby to (try and) deal with and wouldn't have the same time to spend supporting Zoe.

By now the 'Baby Blues' had progressed to Post Natal Depression (PND) but I was still trying to go 'under the radar' and pretend that everything was 'fine'. There was a week when I took Ali for the regular weigh-in/check-up and the clinic nurse sternly said "I don't want to see Ali next week but I want to see you". In my heart I knew why. The next week though, I put on lipstick, smartened myself up by wearing an ironed shirt and feigned being in control. How silly in hindsight.

The words "Incompetent Mother" rang in my ears continually but I tried hard to prove that insensitive nurse wrong, especially in front of Zoe. My memory of that time is pretty fuzzy other than being stressed. I was supposed to feel love for my beautiful new baby and I felt nothing. Absolutely nothing. I could acknowledge that he was a fine looking specimen but that was as far as it went. In fact, I didn't have any feelings for Veli or anyone. I felt numb. All the time.

My memory seemed non-existent and I couldn't think straight. I worried so much I might go out and forget to take

Ali with me that I put a sticky note on the car dashboard to remind me! This may seem odd but it was a little awkward putting him in the car in our garage so I would drive from the parking spot around to the front of the house. I forgot other things too so made copious lists. I was out of the habit of strictly following a diary as I used to need to do.

I managed to last four months and get on a plane so I could show my baby off to everyone in the The Village. I think I was looking forward to a rest and some support but that was somewhat limited, so really life was in fact harder when I was out of my home routine. Veli came for three weeks, then returned to work.

I had arranged to do a UK tour driving Ali and I around to introduce him to family and friends. In hindsight that was an idealistic crazy idea, but I didn't know that when I planned it. I remember coming off the motorway in Somerset, parking by the side of the road, locking the doors and crying myself to sleep as I was too exhausted to drive us safely without a rest.

Another friend, who wanted to do some European travelling came and stayed for a bit and was to help me for the return plane journey but that became an extra pressure too. I wanted to be the tour guide and show her a good time, even though I was mentally not in a position to do so. Another additional pressure existed because she smoked. During the day she was happy to stand by the back door, but at night, tried to do so leaning out of the bedroom window and hope no one would notice! The parentals were not happy and neither was I.

Two other notable things happened at this time. Firstly my left wrist hurt so much, every time I picked Ali up, that I could hardly bear to do so. My brother-in-law Robin was a physiotherapist and suggested I had tendonitis from the way I was handling Ali, so he gave me a few treatments and organised a wrist splint.

Secondly, I was now mentally so low, that I knew I couldn't go on. I had one of my many "How to look after a baby" books with me – we didn't have the internet and Google back then – and read two things of interest. Firstly that "No matter what is going on there is no such thing as the perfect mother but you are the perfect mother for your baby". Then I read the chapter about looking after me. Realising I had PND, I rang Veli to ask him to make a doctor's appointment for me for as soon as I got home.

That he did and I would officially join the ranks of those with a mental health disorder. I say officially because perhaps there had been moments in the past, such as the Karma Chameleon era, when it wasn't diagnosed because I didn't seek help but once you surrender to antidepressants, there's no hiding being a statistic.

As an aside, about eighteen months after my hospital stay, I decided that I needed closure with the hospital and wrote a long letter, airing my grievances. I got a reply thanking me for my feedback, saying they had taken action on a couple of things and to let them know before my next baby so they could give me special attention. I was grateful for this and the fact they were trying to re-gain some credibility but unfortunately by then I had decided not to 'go again'. Due to the time it took to recover from the PND (and later PTSD), the age of Veli and my increased chances of a mental relapse, I thought I didn't have the capacity for another baby.

10: *Shhhhh!* Don't Tell Anyone!

**Versus, if people talked about this,
it would be so much easier**

Being diagnosed with a mental health issue really is a double-edged sword. On the one hand a label is really useful because it means you can receive appropriate help to recover – yes, complete recovery is possible – and on the other hand, you find yourself suffering alone and smiling anyway because of the stigma attached. Oh, and then there may be other issues down the track such as exclusions on insurance policies... Yes really!

Initially I suffered in silence, for a whole six months. In hindsight that didn't serve me, or my baby, or anyone for that matter. Once I had been to the doctor and had PND confirmed there was some sadness but more importantly some relief: I wasn't going mad... I was actually sick and needed support to get better.

Support came in many forms. Everyone is different and this was *my* 'recipe for recovery'. Not that I was reading it from a recipe book, or even the internet because that wasn't so prevalent. Just because this is what worked for me, it doesn't mean it is the formula that would work in exactly the same way for anyone else, but my sincere hope is that it will at least be a thought provoking set of ideas or conversation starters.

When I visited my GP Dr Betty, I left with two pieces of paper: a referral to a psychiatrist and a prescription for Prozac[22]. It was a few weeks before I could see the specialist and in that time I would get some relief from the medication. The reality was that I already started to feel a little better. It was somewhat reassuring to know what I was dealing with and that I actually was sick! Not sick like the sniffles or measles or a broken arm; they would happen at other times in my life, but *sick* nevertheless.

For me, the concept of 'being sick' meant I was ok to medicate based on the doctor's prescription and within a fortnight, I started to feel better because of the antidepressants. I couldn't believe that having a baby – that *thing* I'd wanted to have for as long as I could remember – had made me this way. I knew my life was going to be turned upside down in so many other ways but wasn't expecting to feel like a complete 'basket case', whatever that is. I knew

---

[22] Prozac is a tradename for fluoxetine which is an antidepressant of the selective serotonin reuptake inhibitor (SSRI) class.

I'd be sleep deprived, miss my friends at work and not have dinner parties so easily but still having 'placenta dementia'[23] when I didn't have a placenta anymore, was not in my plan.

After a few weeks I went to the psychiatrist first recommended by Dr Betty. I can't remember her name and it was a struggle going all the way across town for the appointments, especially as I didn't really like her. Not that I *had* to like her but I thought it would help. I certainly felt that I needed to believe in her professional judgement and respect her. I went several times before she completely upset me. I don't recall what she said but I do clearly remember "Have you ever actually *had* a baby?" being my response to one of her questions. She had suggested I do something that seemed completely ridiculous, so I lost faith and didn't go back.

I was referred to another psychiatrist who happened to be much closer to home but, of course I had to wait a few more weeks for an appointment with Dr Tom George.

Somewhere along the way I gathered that he was English because he sounded English. I didn't know he was of Indian descent until I saw him and he offered to make me a cup of tea. Yes *he* went to the kitchen and made the tea! I couldn't believe it. It certainly changed the dynamics and made me feel special. And that was a terrific start.

He was the loveliest man who also happened to be the President of the Marcé Society of Australasia[24] [xxiii] and that

---

23 A 'Jo-ism' for my foggy mind whilst pregnant.
24 The Marcé Society for Perinatal Mental Health is dedicated to supporting research and assistance surrounding prenatal and postpartum mental health for mothers, fathers and their babies.

told me that he really knew his stuff. I was thrilled to be in the care of someone who had a special interest in prenatal and postpartum mental health and was part of various research projects about it. Perfect!

What his extra interest in this area of mental health revealed to me though was that I was suffering from *post traumatic stress disorder* (PTSD) rather than postnatal depression (PND).

How could that be?

I learned that there are cases where mothers are traumatised by a hideous birth experience. Whilst I had very mixed feelings around my stay in the Wesley Hospital, some of which are described in the 'Incompetent Mother' chapter, the birth itself, even though it was a middle-of-the-night 'emergency', didn't seem traumatic to me; I recall taking it in my stride.

In my case, the 'traumatic stress' flashbacks were to my previous experience of parenting Zoe even though she was a teenager not a baby! Wow! Despite my best attempts to 'mother' her the very best way that I could, I actually spent much of my time during those years completely terrified. Being nice to her was the only thing I knew how to do because growing up in The Village didn't arm me with the skills to deal with some of the words that came out of her mouth.

The sad thing was, (and I knew this at the time), the words were Filomena's not hers. Or from the movies. A twelve year old doesn't just say things like: "If you ever lay a finger on me, mother will arrange to have a hit-man shoot you in your sleep."

On another occasion, when Veli actually spoke with Filomena about a particular challenge we were having with Zoe, she replied "A bullet costs $20,000". At the time I clearly recall this being the worst day of my life. Veli pretended not to worry about such statements but it bothered me greatly that people could talk in such terms. If they could forge documents and steal land, then perhaps there was an element of possibility. Or so I thought at the time.

For years we slept with the bedroom door locked and there were many times when I felt like a prisoner in my own home. When Zoe was in a mood, I felt that any sort of destruction was possible, so tried to limit the opportunities for her to be alone in the house. It was no way to live.

Working through those flashbacks with Dr George was tough and rewarding at the same time. But Prozac and 'psyche' sessions with Cognitive Behavioural Therapy[xxiv] (CBT) weren't enough. I had experienced many years of psychological distress and often had physical symptoms too. There were times when my scalp oozed fluid and my clothes were stained from other medication for hideous psoriasis[25].

We had a multi-pronged approach to get me better and that actually took several years. For a few months I went weekly to group therapy sessions at Belmont Private Hospital. An important part of this was simply being

---

25 Psoriasis is a long-lasting autoimmune disease of the skin which is triggered by stress.

around other mothers who were all experiencing their own versions of what I was going through. I was grateful for Veli's support with this. I recall after the first day, we were given information about an evening event for partners. Out of about a dozen in the group, I think only three partners went along and one of those only stayed for a few minutes. At least Veli was interested in how I was trying to get better.

At that time, another symptom I had was no apparent love for him, Ali or anyone in fact. I was emotionless. I knew Ali was a handsome baby but I didn't *feel* anything for him. I was existing on 'mothering autopilot'. Somehow.

I remember the moment that everything changed. I was driving along trying to cheer myself up by listening to music on the radio and when the song "I've Finally Found Someone" by Bryan Adams and Barbara Streisand came on. Not that I was particularly a Bryan Adams fan but the words spoke to me. I felt a warm glow and experienced a glimmer of hope that perhaps I did still love Veli after all. And that was *huge*!

And if I still loved my husband then hopefully I would *feel* love for my baby. To be completely honest I have no recollection of exactly when *that* feeling returned...

One of the things that I heard from a variety of sources was that exercise would be good for me. But I was never *sporty*. What I could do though was walk, and as we lived on the top of a hill this proved to be quite a good exercise workout. And that probably helped me sleep better too. When you're depressed, lying awake at night is especially disturbing, so having a reason for deliberately going to bed earlier was useful.

Something else that I think was beneficial for me was journaling. Writing. Not necessarily words to be re-read but words to be *written*. Quickly. I would sit in the lounge with a little notebook, take some deep breaths and then just started. And carried on. Sometimes I'd set the timer for five or ten or fifteen minutes and sometimes not. The point wasn't to write a thesis that made sense but just get the words out of my head as soon as they entered. No punctuation necessarily. Just what I was feeling about *anything*.

There are more structured forms of journaling where you deliberately write your emotions and thoughts every day but that wasn't my style at that time. Some people write at the same time every day and, as one side effect may be to induce sleep, doing so before bedtime may be helpful.

I've always eaten 'good' food cooked from scratch; not being one to use ready-made meals from the supermarket. I have a huge cook book library and used to enjoy making different dishes from them. Despondency that started in this era led me to ignore them for years but one thing I did take an extra interest in was the mind-food connection: that there are foods than can actually make you *feel* better! One of the books I poured over was *"The Food Doctor – Healing foods for the mind and body"*[26] by Vicki Edgson & Ian Marber. I've always drunk a lot of water so, usually, don't need reminding that that is a good thing to add to the 'feel better' list.

---

[26] Full book details are listed in the chapter 'Jo's Recovery Reading'.

The most surprising part of all this happening in my life, was that it happened in secret. Mostly. I certainly didn't want the parentals to be worried as I thought there was little they could do to help me from The Village. I gave myself an extra stress with this as I had to avoid talking about certain things over the phone! There were a handful of close friends who knew what was going on but usually I suffered in silence. My friends did things like suggesting having a facial or massage and I was so grateful that sometimes they even came to look after Ali so that I could do that more easily.

A constant source of help was my acupuncturist Hermann Weise. I had been seeing him for a few years before and during my pregnancy. Once I was mentally sick he included extras from his 'toolbox of tricks' to support my journey back to optimum health. As well as acupuncture, he had studied the full range of Traditional Chinese Medicine[xxv] (TCM) modalities that included herbs and massage, but for me the 'icing on the cake' was, (and still is) his way with words.

Hermann and I just 'click' and over the years have become good friends as well. But when we meet at the clinic, it's all about helping me to be the best I can be. In every sense. He acknowledged my need for Prozac and in time we openly talked about a plan to come off it to be more 'natural'[27]. This actually took a couple of years though and, of course, was done in conjunction with the guidance of Dr George.

---

27 *Medical disclaimer:* whilst my circumstances are described here, please consult your own doctor or health care practitioner before making any decisions about your own situation.

Hermann had a very different but complementary approach to counselling from Dr George or the CBT at the hospital. I had previously been interested in psychology as a module of my Business Studies at Bristol and I followed Hermann's interest in the teachings of Carl Gustav Jung[xxvi]. This took on a whole new intensity though and whilst I'm a slow reader I was hungry to try and understand from the inside out; what was going on in my head.

I came to accept that all was perfect in my world and that 'Everything happens for a reason'. I'm now a big believer in 'the universe' and synchronicity. Not that I wasn't before, but now there was some theory around the things that I had noticed. I don't 'do God' as such, that's a very personal thing and I leave everyone to come to their own conclusions about, but what I do believe in is the connectedness of everything. And I mean *everything*.

I won't go into detail here about all the books I read – the ones still on my shelf that I can remember nearly two decades later were impactful are listed in the back of this book under the heading of *Jo's Recovery Reading* – but one that did resonate was about why meditation is important. Not *how* to do it but why?

'*Learning to Dance Inside*'[28] by George Fowler is a little book I purchased on a whim in a work lunch break, at the bargain bookshop underneath my building in the city.

This George was a former Trappist monk and despite my previous statement about my relationship with God, I

---

28 Full book details are listed in the chapter 'Jo's Recovery Reading'.

completely loved this petite tome and read it several times. Then I loaned it to a couple of friends who also enjoyed it, and I have re-read it a number of times over the years. The whole meditation idea tied in beautifully with the Jungian theory of the connectedness of all things and the synchronicities in my life. Again and again.

11: Working Through It

Yes, I worked – as in paid employment - through my PTSD... kind of... some of the time...

When Ali was born, I took nine months of maternity leave and then went back three days a week. I didn't return to my previous favourite job though. I say 'favourite' because in the fourteen years working for a Brisbane computer software developer, I had many roles. Those two days of temporary administration work led to me feeling at home and like part of the furniture.

When I was in my favourite role, I flew around Australia to support teams of people in customer service roles, with the implementation of their new case/customer management system that we had supplied. I loved being the trainer/facilitator despite the fact that sometimes there were people in the room whose first preference was to be somewhere else! There was a Sydney bank, a few Victorian councils and a transport authority amongst others. However they were mostly ombudsmen and call centre team members who, because *their* main role was taking (mostly) complaints from the public about a bureaucratic problem, they were nice people to be around. And I made a difference. Someone even described me as "the public face" of the company, which I was proud of.

That wasn't a role that could be done part-time with a baby though.

Another thing that happened was the company was no longer 'A little Brisbane-based software house'. Whilst I was on maternity leave, it became a Canadian one. Then a few months later, an American one. So instead of being a core member of the 'family' that was a hundred people, I was now one of seven thousand working for an enterprise[xxvii] headquartered in Minneapolis, USA. This brought perks like share options but meant I was now just a tiny dot in the 'dot com'[xxviii] era.

Previously, whilst preparing my training materials, and naturally being a perfectionist – which of itself, apparently, is another personal trait that may increase the risk of clinical depression – I found myself being an informal software tester. When I returned to work, that is where I was placed. 'Tester' was in my job description. I naturally warm to people rather than machines so it wasn't the best fit for me. I tried hard to make it work though. Really hard.

Then there was a role shuffle and I somehow became an official document writer. I'm not too bad at telling stories, although I say so myself, but the style of writing needed to document how computer software worked wasn't really my most favourite thing to do either.

Whilst I made great progress with Prozac, Dr George, Hermann and all the other things I was trying to embrace, I held my job down for a while and then had a relapse and had to have a few months off.

By this time Zoe had actually been gone for a while. We didn't know where to or for how long; she simply hung up the phone on me one day when I queried her plan to drive fifty miles to the Gold Coast in her car, for which I suspected the registration had expired. The sad thing was, during the phone call she had also invited us to join her there for her birthday, but I couldn't get my head around how that would work with a new baby.

Once she left though, we were still reminded of her regularly by the constant phone calls from people she owed money to. We couldn't shy away from paying her car loan because we had guaranteed that debt, but, apart from the telecommunications company, we didn't even know what the other amounts were for. The harassment continued for years and the callers didn't believe that we didn't know where she was.

I was still being traumatised in my mind. After moving on from the hideous 'death threat' type words of the previous decade, now I was still worrying about things like why Zoe only gave me a Christmas gift? *Me.* That wasn't how families in The Village behaved. So, she declined an invitation to spend Christmas with us and a larger group we call our 'Christmas Family', but popped around for breakfast. When she gave a gift to me only I said "What about your father and brother?" to which she replied "Dad has you and he doesn't need anything from me" pointing to Ali.

During my time off work, I spent many hours in my favourite place at home: sitting in my front garden amongst the pink flowers and sometimes, if it was too sunny, under the shade of the frangipani tree. I just sat there looking at the clouds and imagining 'things' from the random shapes. And reading of course, lots of reading. By this time, *"Malignant Sadness: The Anatomy of Depression"*[29] by Lewis Wolpert had been published and it was a book that really spoke to me.

I had just opened it randomly and this is what I saw:

> "Depression always occurs within a social context. Relationships, work, poverty, hopes, children, parents and so on, can all play some role in the generation of a depressive episode. To say that the origin of a depression is multifunctional is merely to say that it is necessary to try and tease out the relative importance of the various influences in a person's life. A great deal of research has therefore focused on life events and on the individual's relationships and position in society.

---

[29] Full book details are listed in the chapter 'Jo's Recovery Reading'.

'Life events' is a rather broad term, used to refer to stressful external changes that are rapid, even sudden, and whose time of occurrence can be given a clear and specific date. A life event involves a substantial change in the life of the individual, related, for example, to bereavement, job change or problems with a partner or children."

So, you could say that I had one or two of those factors going on!

Another factor was my relative isolation from family and lack of support. I had lots of friends, some of whom were close and *like* family but the perfectionist in me rarely asked for help. If someone insisted, then I would probably accept but I didn't very often initiate a request.

Veli didn't deliberately *not* support me at this time but he had his own stresses going on, which flowed through to me. He was disturbed by Zoe's behaviour even though she wasn't living with us anymore.

Whilst we had been in the UK on a trip back to The Village, she had – as many teenagers would – taken over the house as her own. Probably the biggest invasions of my privacy were when I knew she had slept in our bed and that she had moved a pregnancy test kit, hidden deep in my bathroom drawer to the family bathroom cupboard. I figured she'd been entertaining too, as numerous bottles of spirits were empty, and *all* the glasses and party platters were not as neat as I was used to storing them. As a result in my 'sick' state, I was so fragile that I demanded she move. We helped her move into a share house within a week.

Veli's other main stress was around money. There had been a slowing in his electrical work and he took on a middle-of-the-night cleaning contract for regular income, from one of his electrical clients. Whilst I understood this, it meant that I received no support from him at all when Ali awoke in the night. I was struggling and so lonely. And the darkness wasn't just from the night sky, especially when I learned that Veli wasn't rushing home after work.

Just before Ali turned one year old, my parents visited from The Village. They were with us for my birthday, our wedding anniversary, a Naming Ceremony for Ali, Christmas, his first birthday and New Year. Rather than feeling *helped* by their presence, the perfectionist in me wanted to show them a nice holiday by me waiting on them. The Naming Ceremony was a big deal and Zoe only attended for half an hour. We filled our front garden with friends and love, had a celebrant and an opera-singing friend graced us with a few tunes. I was exhausted though. So exhausted that for the first time I actually fell asleep standing up!

When I was well enough to return to work, my role changed again. This time, my attention to detail became an asset for the new era of Quality Control. I became the Quality Assurance Representative for the Support Team, which meant I had to attend 'Internal Auditor Training'. I tried to apply myself as much as I could in this working environment and for a couple of years enjoyed the responsibility. Two other major things outside my control were happening though: one in my private world and the other in the world as a whole.

Almost without warning, Ali required open-heart surgery. And the 'dot com bubble'[xxix] burst. In my world these things overlapped slightly.

Ali seemed to be a super fit and a mostly happy and healthy child. Because he was an 'only', I went out of my way to socialise him. He went to day care, then kindergarten on the three days I worked and on the other days we usually had play dates. For five years Friday was 'Mother's Group' with Kristina (and her son Darcy), Dana (and her son Radley) and, before they moved to Sydney, Donna (and her son Randall).

When Ali was four he caught a 'flu type' bug. He'd been off kindy for a couple of days and I was concerned when he refused to drink water. I made an appointment to see Dr Deborah (much closer to home than the previously mentioned Dr Betty) because I hoped he'd listen to her about drinking, even if he wasn't going to listen to me. My motherly instinct that had served me so well during the Zoe years had kicked back in and I *knew* I had to take him to the doctor.

Whilst she was checking him, he fainted! It was remarkable because he hadn't seemed *really* sick.

She said she could hear a murmur in his heart "Which was probably nothing to worry about – just more apparent today because of his other bug" but if I wanted it checked further she'd happily supply a referral to a paediatrician. The only thing was, we were due to go overseas to The Village in a couple of weeks. She said rather than it being urgent before we left, it could wait till our return.

After being away, the earliest appointment I could get was for a work day. Because it didn't seem to be *that* important, I let Veli take him. Veli heard firstly that the murmur was confirmed and it was "probably nothing to worry about" but if we wanted to get it checked by a cardiologist then we could.

Again, it didn't seem *so* important that both Veli and I should go, so on this occasion I took him. Dr W went through whether Ali was always last when running with other kids? No! Whether he was often breathless? No again! And then looked at his heart on some sort of machine. I can still recall the words as he leant over to point out some blurry images on the screen. "You see this – we've got to get a plumber in there to fix it" he said. "What do you mean?" was my reply.

Ali had a 1.5 cm hole between the upper chambers of his heart – an atrial septal defect[xxx] (ASD). It could only be repaired by open-heart surgery and the good news was the best person to do it was Dr P at The Prince Charles Hospital which was five minutes from home.

I was stunned. I wanted to cry. I knew I had to be strong in front of Ali. Why wasn't Veli with me? I knew the answer to that question… because we weren't expecting bad news. Ali played with the lift buttons and for once he got away with it, as I cried whilst settling the account. It was a few days before Christmas and his fifth birthday.

It wasn't "Life or death – has to be done next week" surgery but it was "medium urgent". In the lead up to the surgery we didn't really need to change his routine except that when he broke a tooth clambering out of a swimming pool, we couldn't get it fixed in a random orthodontists' rooms; it had to be one with a proper sterile operating theatre!

I took time off work and on the Wednesday before Easter we arrived early at the hospital. We scored a great day because it was the (then) monthly visit by the Starlight Foundation[xxxi]. Ali had his face painted as Spiderman and generally had lots of fun to distract him. Veli and I on the other hand, were eagerly awaiting the appointment with Dr P which actually didn't happen until very late at night because another baby's surgery was more complicated than first thought.

I spent the night at the hospital in a reclining chair next to Ali's bed and after giving him a special pre-surgery bath we went off to the operating theatre. Veli and I waited what seemed like all day but it was only a few hours. The procedure went well but we were amazed to learn that the hole had actually been 2.5 cm! In the few months since diagnosis it had grown. That would be a big hole in an adult but in my little boy it was absolutely *huge*.

After being in the intensive care unit for about 24 hours, he moved to a ward. On Saturday, the Easter Bunny visited and Ali was cheered up by lots of chocolate gifts donated by local businesses. On Easter Sunday he was checked and, given we literally lived five minutes away and could see the hospital from our front garden, was discharged on condition we returned if we had any concerns. It was a miracle that less than one hundred hours after arriving for open-heart surgery Ali was back at home! Very weak but happy to be home.

I spent a couple of weeks caring for Ali at home until he was strong enough to go back to kindy. It had been an incredibly emotional time and we were comforted that everything had gone smoothly. Work became stressful though because in the previous few months the company had been shedding employees by the thousand. The goal was to move from an enterprise of 7,000 to one of 5,000. My role had become redundant and in my termination interview I learned that they kept me on for a few extra weeks so that I didn't have something else to worry about *before* Ali's surgery. For that I was extremely grateful.

12: A Star is Born – But It's Not as Shiny as it Could Be

So, fourteen years after Ali was born, I found myself in a position where my corporate job had been made redundant and I missed putting on my lipstick and heels, even if it was for just three days a week. A few changes presented themselves in the shape of a multi-level marketing business. It turned out that I excelled at selling books for children and built a successful business with it. I was given an interesting gift at the company's annual conference for being the top seller in Australia and New Zealand combined: a named star in the sky called "Jo Hassan's Piece of Heaven" (in the Corona Australis).

Life didn't feel so heavenly though as selling books and the associated deliveries and paperwork was actually a lot of work. Not super *hard* work but some of it was low-level drudgery compared to other roles I had held: and I didn't earn enough to be able to delegate and pay anyone else to do the tasks I didn't enjoy

What it did though, was pave the way for hard work of a different kind, so that when another opportunity came up to join with a friend in creating a pet resort, I felt totally ready to tackle the challenge.

Sam and I had worked together for the IT company. In fact, I played a part in employing her because she'd done a thesis on 'customer satisfaction measurement' and that fitted in perfectly with the software we were developing and in which I trained clients how to use. We became good friends just before she fell pregnant, so much so that I was actually at the hospital when her son Zane was born – waiting in the next room with her mother. Nine months later Ali was born and they saw so much of each other, for years Ali actually told people Zane was his brother!

Sam decided on a 'sea change' and moved to the Sunshine Coast sixty-five miles north of Brisbane, to buy a dog kennel business. Along the way she had another son, created a cattery on the neighbouring block of land and then had a marriage break-up. During discussions around that, I said: "Well we could buy Virgil's share of the business". And so we did. Kind of.

We talked about creating a pet resort, a one stop shop so cats and dogs could holiday, get vaccinated, groomed and even buried in a pet cemetery. We looked at blocks of land and learned lots about town planning and 'change of use'.

Along the way we found a third partner in Will, a retired Canadian jumbo pilot, bought another pet motel that was for sale and consolidated the three operations with the metaphor that we were *taking three fish and chip shops and creating a seafood restaurant*.

We tried. In fact, we tried really hard! Will also had a marriage break-up that contributed to a difference of opinion, especially around goals like the pet cemetery and unfortunately, he became so difficult to work with that we had a partnership breakdown that cost us significant money in legal fees. No sooner was the ink dry on that partnership dissolution than Sam unfortunately had a really serious mental health issue herself, which meant *we* could no longer work together either... so a few more years of extreme stress and legal discussions.

Despite the decline in the relationship between Sam and me, it's wonderful that Zane and Ali are still close, like brothers as they have been their whole lives.

In the early years of the Pet Resort Partnership (PRP), Sam and I thrived on our chalk-and-cheese differences: she was all about the big picture where I was always focused on the details. She was the animal lover and I was the strategic outsider questioning 'Why?' We loved one another like sisters and she even introduced me to people as her 'sister from another mother'.

The business struggled though and the only good thing was that we knew it! My resilience was certainly being tested again. We sought guidance from a business which coached methodology, instantly embraced those ideas, took action on tasks and could see immediate results which made me feel stronger. We even won an award!

What we weren't expecting was that the coaching support would eventually be withdrawn from us because rather than continue, the coaching company planned to focus instead, on selling franchises in their business model!

I saw a great opportunity in that because there was an overlap between the training and facilitation role I had had in IT, which I really enjoyed, especially with learning and sharing these new ideas. To me it was just a different audience - mostly business owners instead of call centre team members. Also we had proven that a lot of their material worked in our pet resort business, especially around systems.

This led to my becoming a Red Day Coaching® Partner, which did overlap with my involvement with the PRP business. Whilst I had lots of success stories from other clients around Australia, I had a continual flow of examples that were closer to home.

By this time Ali was declared *normal* with respect to his heart. He was a taekwondo black belt, a keen drummer, interested in perfecting BMX stunts at the skate park, enjoying high school and being world champion in the (fledgling in Australia) sport of footbiking[30]. I also enjoyed being the mother who could be flexible around working hours and attend school sports day and tuck shop as well as

---

30   A footbike is like an adult scooter with bicycle wheels.

the Mother's Spring Luncheon and all those nice add-ons to parenting.

Sometimes though, the parenting and being 'Business Superwoman' was *really* hard and I would feel like I had regressed back into a version of depression. It's hard for anyone being in the middle of a situation involving lawyers (which sadly I ended up having to do when selling out of the PRP business), but to do so and maintain a public image of everything being 'fine' was stressful in itself. It probably wasn't PTSD again but definitely far more serious than just having an 'off' day.

After a couple of years taking the antidepressant Prozac, and then a couple of years off it, I did go back on it when Ali was about five, for a while. Then, what I worked out over the years was when I started to feel low, the time period from then to when I felt somewhat improved, lessened. Whilst I've taken St John's wort (an over-the-counter herbal or more natural remedy for depression) on a number of occasions, I've resisted getting a medical prescription again[31].

When things seem like they are about to fall down around me, I now notice it sooner and find myself making observations like; "Why have I been too busy to exercise? Or why am I going to bed so late? Or why haven't I been eating much fruit?" The mere fact that I'm asking myself these questions, gives the mind a little jolt along to re-frame itself.

---

31 *Medical disclaimer:* whilst my circumstances are described here, please consult your own doctor or health care practitioner before making any decisions about your own situation.

So it seems like I'm on a continuous journey to happiness and feeling in *control*, as I guess we *all* are.

My recovery from PTSD has been mostly steady and in the right direction, although this diagram does show some valleys that get pretty deep and dark.

Perhaps there's a sliding scale where at one extreme the PTSD sufferer is completely debilitated and unable to control much of their life: the middle valley in the diagram above. At either side there are other stages: on the left where there's a (perhaps) undiagnosed struggle and hint of mental illness and on the far right where there's a belief of complete control and you're as good as you're going to get! The left is the time *before* diagnosis (my Karma Chameleon era), or before a label, or in my case before 'the trauma' when perhaps there were symptoms of depression that went undiagnosed because I didn't seek professional help. Help for such things, even now nearly forty years later, I suspect wouldn't be found in The Village anyway.

For the last few years I've found myself saying 'smile anyway'. Not that I'm advocating to smile and keep depression a secret and not get help – as I did twenty years ago – or that smiling alone can change your circumstances in a hurry. More that some things are going to happen that are not so good and dwelling on that puts the mind in a sadder place than thinking about possible good notions from *anything*. I mean *anything*. And be grateful!

Gratitude has been huge for me for many years. Before getting out of bed in the morning and before going to sleep I try to remember to say five things I'm grateful for out loud. Yes... out loud. So I can hear my own words. During the day I will say 'Thank you' when I get a perfect parking spot or when I want the traffic light to stay green long enough for me to get through. And it usually does!

And I celebrate wins. Little ones as well as big ones. This is subtly different to being grateful – which I am, of course, as well when I have a win.

As smiling became a habit, I confirmed something that I always knew – that being around negative or toxic people didn't feel good. Sometimes it's unavoidable but when I did have a choice, I would generally choose to not be there. I don't mean of course that when a friend had a crisis I didn't support them but more choosing to spend less time with people who are habitually negative, 'glass half empty' or putting me down.

I also noticed that I only wanted to be with depressed people or talk about depression *sometimes*. It was perfect as part of my formal therapy to recover but when, without the safety net of the 'four walls' of the therapeutic situation, I found talking about it actually made me feel tight-chested and stressed: so *worse*! Choosing who I spent my time with therefore became more important than ever.

Writing is extremely powerful too and quite often I'll write a list of one hundred things I'm grateful for. They don't have to be *huge* things, although some might be. Another nice idea that I do sometimes is have a Gratitude Jar. It's filled with dated pieces of paper and the best thing that happened on that day. This means that on a day when things are not going so well, I can pick out a lucky dip and cheer myself up by reading something that previously made me happy. Believe it or not, it's an accumulation of the *little things* that can move you along the journey to 'control'. And back. And back and forth in both directions, yo-yoing through life's ups and downs.

If you follow the dotted line in the diagram you can see that sometimes there is a 'two steps forward, three (or more) step back' scenario as you move from the depths of PTSD towards Control.

You come to realise that perhaps you will always have to manage your 'state' in the same way that someone living with, for example, diabetes does. In time – hopefully – you are *generally* more in control more of the time and the variations from one extreme to the other are less pronounced.

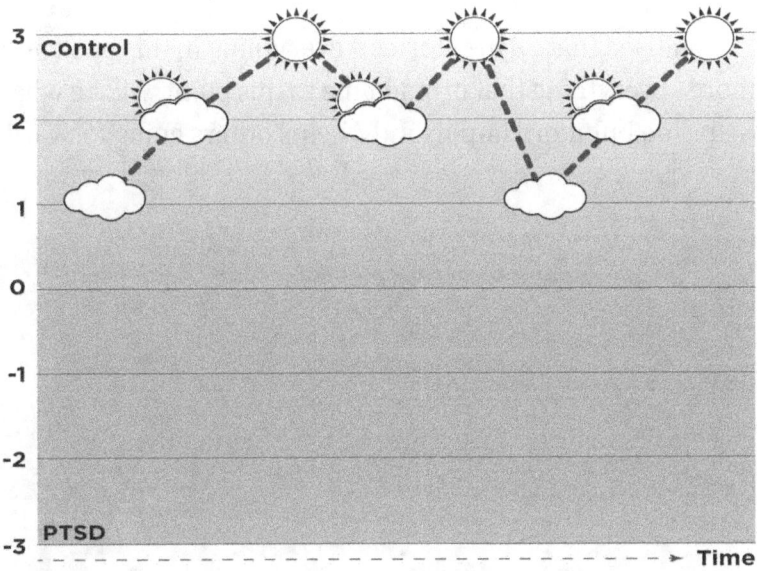

Rather than dwelling on feeling like a victim, you are better served by trying to live life on a more even keel. That's not to say that you don't celebrate a big win with exuberance or are not devastated if someone you know is seriously injured in an accident, but rather you don't stay in that place for so long to distort your longer term view of the world.

A possible reason for my 'smile anyway' coping mechanism in the last few years is that I've had to put on a brave face with my coaching clients as my income depended on that. As my confidence in myself and my ability to support others has grown, in recent years sharing some of what's going on (or went on) has become part of my authenticity that I believe is liked and respected. Eventually it became a better option for me to evolve into my own brand of coaching and I moved away from the Red Day Coaching® franchise, creating instead my own PinkWise® brand.

I realised that all the stories – everything in this book and more - everything that brought me to this point, will be what helps me but more importantly, helps others going forward.

13: Becoming PinkWise®

Apart from being with people I love, two things are guaranteed to naturally put a smile on my face: listening to "Dancing Queen" by Abba and seeing hot pink/magenta/fuchsia (almost) anything. It's my 'go to' colour for friends for any gift, I wear it completely or accessorise with it, just about every day and in the house that I lived in for twenty-six, years, even the sail on the deck was that colour.

I've enjoyed it my whole life but only had an addiction for about two decades! I recall my 16th, 18th and 21st birthdays were decorated in pink. Even my bridesmaid frocks were 'shocking pink' as it was called back then. When I turned thirty, guests were invited to wear pink to my party where even the food was that colour and for some, if they didn't already have it in their wardrobe, it was a real challenge. I do recall though, that since then, it has been much easier as it has been a fashion colour every year or two.

When it was time to re-think my business recently I gathered a trusty group of associates together and the main thing they agreed on in the first meeting was the colour pink had to be involved somehow. How bizarre. But then 'how normal' when you know that it's *me* you're talking about! The special day that we called a PinkTank® was facilitated by a public relations expert and attended by a marketing and website expert, a trusted friend who happens to have a psychology qualification, a team member and myself. For my part before they arrived I transformed an ordinary meeting room into a 'pink wonderland' with as much pink as I could easily gather together. This included tablecloths, fairy lights, tinsel, flamingos, cut out hearts and other random objects such as hats, suit, suitcases, beads, rose quartz and much more. I really loved this process and then seeing everyone's smiling faces as they walked through the door. Someone said it felt like walking into Disneyland!

PinkWise® was the name we settled on and I felt completely comfortable with that even though interestingly, I probably had more male than female clients. Historically though, pink actually used to be a *male* colour and blue a female one[xxxii.] How times change...

No one in the room knew about my PTSD history and these are unedited lists straight from the whiteboard.

"**What makes Jo awesome:**

- Fairy godmother
- Gutsy, empathy, confidence, open arms (qualities of a champion and elite athlete)
- Romantic

- Nurturing
- Personal value of fairness
- Not impulsive
- Hardworking and diligent
- Bring heart
- Nurturing energy
- Supportive
- Can bring action to vision
- Long-term strategic (thoughtful considered)
- Organise and pull people together
- Ability to see things
- Jo's finishing school
- Dream-motivator
- Fun
- Modern mother role model

Stuff Jo loves doing – is good at – would like to do more of:

- Facilitating groups
- Connecting people
- Working the room
- Making personal connections
- Creating atmosphere and energy
- Bringing business people together in a supportive environment and facilitating outcomes without a fixed agenda or model

- Systems Queen
- Creating real successes for people on a personal level, helping them have better personal and family lives
- Leading by example, walking the walk
- Ability to dig in and get to the root of a problem
- Believing in and supporting people
- Enabling people without dictating to them what they have to do
- Collaborating and not controlling
- Working to people's strengths"

It is quite a list to live up to and I'm still a 'work in progress'! And, the people who comprised this list only know the 'smile anyway happy Pink Jo'. Not the Jo who seriously worked on herself for nearly two decades and struggled for a decade or two before that. It's time to 'bring her out' and show that it is possible to recover from PTSD. At least mostly.

It's also time to have a discussion and share and not hide behind the taboos any more. If more people talked about mental illness, then others wouldn't be so embarrassed to admit they needed help. After all, if this could happen to me, it could truly happen to anyone.

The irony now is, as I'm in my sixth decade, I'm so grateful for the 'gift of growing up'. I guess I only know how it has been and that is obviously what shaped who I am today. I don't dwell on the sadness and extreme stress of some aspects of my past and with hindsight wouldn't change a thing. I only *know* the *me* that I am, and that's the one who is called "Pink Jo" by many.

So my personal small business experience thus far – from Pa's motor cycle shop, to Veli's electrical service, to the 'children's bookstore', to the Pet Resort to Red Day Coaching® and then PinkWise® – led me to believe that business won't work unless there is heart in it. People buy people and especially when they believe they help solve a problem for them. People who *believe* in what they are selling, regardless of whether it is a product or service, are more connected and happier. Happier people are *much* nicer to be around and sell more.

Most small business owners start out as technicians because they excelled at a particular skill such as plumbing or fixing computers, or had a passion for something like baking cakes or garden design. It's all really exciting in the beginning and they don't even mind doing all the peripheral tasks like answering the phone, ordering stock or doing their own invoices. Because (they think) they're 'saving money' and it's 'all for them'.

What happens though is they get busy. *Really* busy. Busier than they've ever been in their life. They become overwhelmed, tired, and often broke. They see their family even less than they did before despite 'working around the family' being one of the motivators for becoming the entrepreneur.

At this point they may have some kind of breakdown or mid-life crisis or depression. If they have enough insight to know they need help with their business, they might seek out the services of an organisation like PinkWise®. Sometimes well-meaning friends and family suggest they do so. But more often than not they suffer in silence, because just as there is probably still public stigma around depression and PTSD, there are also myths that small business owners are supposed to know what they are doing. Asking for help doesn't come naturally to many!

Small business owners might feel comfortable sharing their woes with others like themselves. However, if they are at a social event with mostly employees, who generally have no idea of life 'on the other side', they will probably suffer from embarrassment, if asked to reveal any problem. So, they will probably remain silent or fake a response and say "Everything's fine" when asked, even if it isn't. I know how this feels! And, if things are bad enough, they won't even attend the event – they'll stay home. I know how this feels too.

Over the years I've had a few clients who I've sent to their doctor... suggesting that they *may* have clinical depression[32]... and that perhaps they need to start working on that before I can help them with their business. One man even thanked me for saving his life by me taking this approach. I don't ever profess to be a counsellor and I may or may not reveal

---

32 *Medical disclaimer:* I am not a doctor or health care practitioner but I have been called an empath and a great listener. Please seek your own medical support if my personal story resonates enough that you feel you too could benefit from external assistance.

that I have had PTSD and clinical depression myself, but what I am able to do often, is recognise it in others and put a label on it that may not have occurred to them previously. I guess it's that nurturing or mothering 'sixth sense' kicking in again that served me so well in the past with Zoe. The clients have known they're 'not right' but haven't had the impetus to go to the doctor previously of their own volition. If I can fast-track them to getting medical help, then I've served my purpose of helping already. As the state of the business is a reflection of the person, then that's usually the start of longer term business improvement too. I say 'longer term' because it almost always does not improve over night, although aspects of it can.

So talking of 'purpose': I believe if a business is following its purpose then it will do a better job if everyone knows what that purpose is and 'lives' it. If it's a *small* business where the owner is intimately involved then the 'owner's purpose' will have to be fulfilled as well.

The Dalai Lama said: "The purpose of our lives is to be happy." Everyone will have a different take on this but purpose can include concepts like working towards a particular goal or plan, being empowered to fulfil a dream or your motivation for starting the business. This also has to work in with your personal values.

Aside from this, writing down your goals is an incredibly powerful exercise. It's been proven in studies many times[33]

---

33 Most notably at the USA Universities of Yale and Harvard in 1953 and 1979 respectively.

that writing down your goals increases their chance of being realised. There is magic in picking up a pen and writing as it connects the right and left sides of the brain: creativity and order are brought together, which makes it easier for the brain to look out for signals that help you achieve whatever the goal is.

Over the years I've come to realise how important 'energy' is too. The Oxford English Dictionary defines it as "1. force, vigour, capacity for activity. 2. individual powers in use. 3. *Physics* the capacity of matter or radiation to do work."

Energy is connected to your spirit or the 'vibe', and your energy is intrinsically linked to your happiness. People often describe me as vibrant; and I *really* mean often! I find that somewhat unusual because it's not a word that everyone uses every day. For me I'm thinking it ties in with my 'smile anyway' policy: a kind of effervescence. That doesn't mean that everyone has to be bubbly and active all the time.

It does mean though that 'the power is turned on', even if on 'low' or 'sleep'. If you find this hard, then meditating may help as it did for me. In *"Learning To Dance Inside"*[34] by George Fowler, he states:

> "Meditation is a way of correcting the fact that human formation customarily teaches our minds to chatter about the world of appearances, but never trains them to give us an adequate grasp of the unseen – and greater – reality in which we live.

---

34   Full book details are listed in the chapter 'Jo's Recovery Reading'.

Meditation is a means of coming to an experience of this greater reality.

The mind would have us believe that what it perceives through the senses, is all there is to our universe. Thousands of years of human spiritual experience, however – as well as our own occasional moments of intuition – suggest there is more. Meditation is a way of finding this more for ourselves, not by better thinking, but by learning to go beyond the mind and its limitations and to seek a non-conceptual experience of what thought alone has failed to give us."

Having energy also means that you're healthy and vital and can get in your flow to create efficiencies in your business and life, and to have fun. And having *fun* is really important. Or at least regularly participating in activities that give you pleasure.

What gives you pleasure is up to you to decide. Jane Austen said "One half of the world cannot understand the pleasures of the other". I've mentioned previously how important gratitude has become for me and it's hard to be truly grateful and to not find that enjoyable.

I'd like to think that everyone can find some pleasure every day in some form. It might be a little (or big) treat, it might be giving or receiving love or affection or it could be experiencing a beautiful sunrise or sunset with wonderment. If you can find pleasure whilst working, then that is good for absolutely everyone, including the customers.

If you're a business owner then profit is vitally important. If you're an employee then your 'profit' is instead your take home pay. For others it might be that any surplus over what's needed is given away in acts of philanthropy and that in itself gives one a feeling of abundance or prosperity. Freedom might be your *big* goal as a benefit from income and assets.

My many years of supporting others with the big juggle of personal, family and business life has led me to come up with a term I call PEPP® as an indicator for goals, progress towards them and decision making. PEPP® is an acronym meaning Purpose, Energy, Pleasure and Profit.

PEPP® is a tool that helps you think about your values before doing any activity. And I mean *any* activity. In business or outside of business.

If the 'thing' that you're doing doesn't fulfil your personal (or your business') purpose, energise you, give you pleasure and/or profit then *why* are you doing it? It's such a cliché now but 'life really *is* short'. So many people just 'exist' rather than living whilst they are alive. That may be because they are living with a mental illness like depression or PTSD. It might be because they are a struggling business owner. It might be because their cat just died, they've recently had a relationship break-up or some other stressful event.

Whatever the reason, some tasks and experiences 'fill up our bucket' and others are a drain. If it's a negative, then my purpose with PEPP® is that you are stopped in your tracks and think about what or how the situation can be handled differently.

When I mentioned it to my friend Shelley recently, she said she doesn't like cooking family meals. I suggested that her children were old enough to have some fun, taking a turn each every week and then perhaps there could be a business goal to increase profit enough to have a more regular dining out or takeaway treat. She reported back that the teenagers were excited by the challenge; so everyone was happy!

Thinking about PEPP® gave Shelley a framework and/or welcome reason to re-think a negative in her life. That truly can only be a good thing because however much we think "I've got this", there will be times when we surprise ourselves, when we actually have slid back into the darkness.

14: The Queen of Resilience

Being resilient was not a descriptor I sought for myself. I simply had to survive an hour, a day, a week, a month... as I did feel an incredible sense of responsibility to look after my new baby. I think that was what drove me. That, and proving I was being a *competent* mother rather than an *incompetent* one! It didn't occur to me that that wasn't how everyone behaved until Dr Tom George said to me "You really are the Queen of Resilience aren't you?" He was just the first; and over the years, it was a phrase a number of other health professionals used including TCM (Traditional Chinese Medicine) healer Hermann Weise.

Interestingly, there is another point of view that being so 'tough and resilient' isn't necessarily such a good thing. I recall a time when, lamenting with a business mentor George about some of the dramas that led to the protracted difficulties and then legal intervention at the Pet Resort, he said "You know Jo, if you weren't so resilient, perhaps you would have sought help sooner or given up sooner". He had studied psychology but had chosen not to practice it, and I guess he was right. That, or I would have fallen back into a complete relapse, to a state where I couldn't function. We will never know.

When I was at my deepest, darkest point with the PTSD, it didn't occur to me to 'not' try to look after my baby. And I never considered deliberately leaving the planet. Well not then anyway! The only time I've ever felt suicidal was in about February 1989 when, after migrating half way around the world, I struggled to find permanent employment. I'd go to job interviews and was way too honest about the fact that I needed a month off, six months after starting, because I had to finesse the plans and attend my English second wedding in The Village. We didn't have the internet and other more 'immediate response' communication tools back then, so I needed more time than just the day itself to finalise the arrangements.

I was desperately sad and lonely – missing my family and hadn't really made any friends yet. I also felt guilty about not contributing financially to our marriage although I should say that I don't recall any pressure from Veli around this: being employed was something I wanted to do to feel valued myself. I recall lying in bed one night, contemplating throwing myself off the balcony. We lived on the third floor. The main reason I didn't do it was because I knew it would make a wreck out of Veli and he would perhaps never recover. I loved him so much I couldn't do that to him. Perhaps falling only three floors wasn't enough to die and then my life would be *even* worse!

So what does 'resilience' even mean? Well the Oxford English Dictionary says "The capacity to recover quickly from difficulties, toughness" or "The ability of a substance or object to spring back into shape, elasticity". According to personality profiling systems, some people are born with a greater capacity to do this and for others it is a learned skill, thank goodness!

Psychological capacity can actually be measured, so therapists may do this before and after a patient has received assistance and the tools to be more resilient.

If I'm naturally resilient, the wiring in my brain in my former years has enabled me to be that way. When I've found myself in difficult situations, my unconscious memory has been able to reflect back in the moment - a bit like a mental bridge from the past to now - and know that it will work out all right. I'm not defeatist but usually optimistic even when experiencing an obstacle. I have an ability to re-frame a novel or new difficult situation by talking to myself. I might actually say out loud "I know I'll get through this" or "I know there'll be better days" and my internal dialogue is (usually) positive.

There have been times when I have literally sung Bob Marley's "Everything's Gonna Be Alright" and often in bed before going to sleep and upon waking. In the past, Prozac may have helped correct a chemical imbalance in the brain but it didn't help with the internal dialogue! This came from effort: being a mental sponge in the company of the various medical and therapeutic counsellors or self-directed learning such as when I read the Jungian psychology books. Apparently many people think that drugs will make them better without them putting any effort in.

I remember when I had an accident and broke the top off my arm a few years ago. I religiously did the physiotherapy exercises at home, to bring me back to almost the same movement capability as before. The surgeon said I had "recovered so well from the hideously debilitating injury" that he wouldn't rush to remove the titanium plate and nine pins he'd inserted, as he couldn't guarantee me any more flexibility. The physiotherapist confirmed several times that most people expect to get better without doing the exercises between appointments. It's the same when it's your mind that is sick: you have to do the 'exercises' and they build a resilience reference point in the mind for the brain to refer to in the future.

Sir Winston Churchill apparently said "Success is the ability to go from one failure to another with no loss of enthusiasm." If that is the benchmark then I certainly have felt like that over the years, and I wouldn't be alone in that regard: "Wear pink and smile anyway!"

Despite Churchill's profound observation around resilience, there were times during his nine years leading the UK that he was seriously depressed or, as he called it, *with the black dog*. Nassir Ghaemi, a Tufts University (A private university founded in the USA in 1852) psychiatry professor said that mentally sound people can lead well when the issues are *normal* but "in times of crisis and tumult, those who are mentally abnormal, even ill, become the greatest leaders. We might call this the Inverse Law of Sanity."[xxxiii]

Apparently normal people have a slightly rosier view of how much they control their environment whereas those living with a mental disorder are more likely to see things as they really are; some things can't be controlled and must simply be dealt with.

How they are dealt with though is where the differences begin. As situations become more unusual or catastrophic and outside the experience of conventional tactics, those who are more familiar with intense highs and deep lows of feeling, draw on that to become more creative. And whilst they may be labelled 'crazy' or 'maverick' that is usually when the genius/new ideas/new decisions appear. That's often when the world moves forward in a fresh and creative way. These leaders have no qualms "Calling a spade a spade" and that can be very refreshing for the masses.

Abraham Lincoln is another leader who suffered greatly from depression and PTSD. He almost drowned when he was seven, his mother died when he was nine, his sister when he was nineteen, his first love before they married and three of his four children passed before he himself was murdered. No wonder he came up with the phrase "and this too shall pass".

Apparent resilience may be seen in many celebrities who've suffered from trauma. The USA television talk show host and author Oprah Winfrey is a case in point. She was raped by a family member when she was just nine years old. As a coping tool she was sexually promiscuous for years and actually had a baby herself who died, when she was just fourteen. No wonder she's such a passionate advocate for survivors of sexual abuse. And kind. And grateful. And generous. In her book "*What I Know For Sure*"[35] her selected quote to describe the word *resilience* is "Barn's burnt down – now I can see the moon" by the seventeenth century Japanese poet Mizuta Masahide.

Not everyone has the capacity to shine continually, whether they are in the public eye or not. When the actor Robin Williams died from suicide in 2015, many were at a loss to understand how someone who brought humour and joy to millions could be so sad internally. The reality is this; the "Wear pink and smile anyway!" system of mine is not for everyone. And even if you wanted to, for some people on some days it's *just too hard*. And, of course, 'pink' is a metaphor for whatever makes *you* happy... *your* heart sing. It might be wearing brown (yes, I know someone who's favourite colour *is* brown) or thinking about your dog!

In "*What I Know For Sure*" Oprah Winfrey says:

> "I know for sure that healing wounds of the past is one of the biggest and most worthwhile challenges of life. It's important to know when and how you were programmed, so you can change the program. And doing so is your responsibility, no one else's. There

---

35 Full book details are listed in the Chapter 'Other Books Referenced'.

is one irrefutable law of the universe. We are each responsible for our own life.

If you're holding anyone else accountable for your happiness, you're wasting your time. You must be fearless enough to give yourself the love you didn't receive. Begin noticing how every day brings a new opportunity for your growth. How buried disagreements with your mother show up in arguments with your spouse. How unconscious feelings of unworthiness appear in everything you do (and don't do). All these experiences are your life's way of urging you to leave the past behind and make yourself whole. Pay attention. Every choice gives you a chance to pave your own road. Keep moving. Full speed ahead."

Mental illness in the form of depression or PTSD is not a prerequisite for requiring resilience. Sometimes continual (apparent) failure requires it too. I'd rather not use the term 'failure' as really it is a vehicle or an opportunity for continual improvement or learnings.

In the business world, Steve Jobs the founder of Apple Inc bounced back after being sacked by his own board in 1985, following a series of product failures[xxxiv]. Sir Richard Branson, in his book "*Losing My Virginity*"[36] describes literally dozens of setbacks – many financial – and he continues to this day to be adventurous and outwardly happy.

---

36 Full book details are listed in the chapter "Other Books Referenced".

Whilst he didn't actually invent the electric lightbulb, Sir Thomas Edison apparently had nearly 1,000 attempts at perfecting it for practical use. He must have been pretty resilient with a steadfast goal of lighting up the world. He even laughed through his workspace burning down due to a chemical explosion. Apparently, according to his son Charles in a 1961 Readers Digest article, he said "Go get your mother and all her friends. They will never see a fire like this again." When Charles protested, Edison replied "It's all right. We've just got rid of a lot of rubbish."[xxxv]

Everyone has a past. *Everyone*. Obviously a fifty year old or an eighty year old has more 'past' than a ten year old. No one lives without 'something' and we can choose to think doom and gloom and dwell on that 'thing'. Or allow it to shape us. We can embrace what's going on or resist and fight against it. It's much harder to fight.

To quote Carl Gustav Jung "I am not what happened to me, I am what I choose to become."

15: "I Am What I Choose To Become"

This book could be summarised in just fourteen words from Carl Gustav Jung: "I am not what happened to me, I am what I choose to become."

I have lived with 'mental illness' for most of my life. Most of the time it doesn't occur to me to think about it. When I have wanted to tick a goal I have never thought "Oh I can't do that because I've had clinical depression or PTSD". Never!

I'm mindful too of a couple of statements made by former Governor General of Australia Dame Quentin Bryce. She said "Taking good care of yourself means building stores of resilience for those tough times." And then "Women need to have the discipline to look after their spiritual, mental and physical health. It's much easier to be a workaholic."[xxxvi] That's a statement that ties in beautifully with my rationale around the need for PEPP® as a decision-making tool. Based on this, sometimes I wonder how my family even survived the continual challenge of dramas that have come our way. Especially given Dr Betty's instructions that it was up to me to "make or break the family". I guess Dame Quentin's words reinforce that.

I have now celebrated thirty years in Australia since coming from The Village with a backpack. I don't know any other life than the shiny one with (sometimes) jagged edges that I've lived. I choose to wear pink and smile anyway regardless of what's going on because that is my sanity saver. Mostly. I have to be happy with the cycle of life's ups and downs because being any other way doesn't serve me or those in any of my 'circles': from family and close friends, to clients, to people I meet along the way and those in my speaking audiences.

I have come to know intimately that PTSD is not just for first responders, people in war zones or those who have experienced physical trauma, but that it affects ordinary 'everyday people' too for extraordinary reasons. I had no idea.

After having a twelve year old suddenly become part of my life and the traumas that it brought both in the moment and much later, I have learned so much about resilience and keeping business and life going, regardless of what else is going on. As with everything I do, both easily and less easily, the experiences add to the richness of life. Instant motherhood was no exception. In fact, there were just as many (more) lessons from parenting the son that I *did* give birth to!

What I cherish now is the opportunity to take these learnings and share them widely. Entrepreneurs and leaders are close to my heart because so many keep mental health challenges a secret and that impacts their families, their teams, their clients and their suppliers. In fact, it affects everyone they come into contact with. And, of course it affects their profit too.

This story is my 'normal'. Hopefully there are some ideas that improve your normal. What's *normal* anyway? Normal is how it is. For everyone.

"I am not what happened to me, I am what I choose to become."

Epilogue

Full Circle, Times Two

I took the words "Till death us do part" in my marriage vows very seriously. Sadly though, after twenty-seven years and a conversation that lasted a whole ninety seconds, Veli and I decided to go our separate ways. That isn't the whole story of course – there were lots of factors and conversations in the lead up to it, but the actual dialogue where we made the decision was literally ninety seconds. In a storm at 10.30 a.m. on 29 December 2015. (I mention the time only because people familiar with sub-tropical Brisbane know that there are rarely storms in the morning!)

We had had a very stressful few years, which included making multiple business decisions we would later regret. Veli's parents had sadly both passed away and were buried together in Kos. There was a requirement that you couldn't put a headstone on a grave for a year and Veli was planning the trip to do this.

I suggested he take his time and not rush home. He knew why. We did rush though when the wind came – from the kitchen to the washing line! We had five lines of dry laundry and hurriedly unpegged and folded so it didn't get wet again. By the time we'd brought it all in I said "I have two requests – I'd like to do *Divorce With Dignity* and spend minimal money on lawyers". He simply said "Agreed and I have two requests – to stay friends with you and stay friends with your family". Of course I said "Agreed".

So that was that. An amazingly weird, quick conversation that I guess was just perfect. We were united after a quick nine day love affair so it was probably a miracle we lasted more than three years let alone nearly three decades.

We were harmonious for most of that time and whilst we miraculously survived the extreme stresses, including PND and PTSD, we sadly grew apart through the business dramas on multiple fronts that defined our last few years together. We have raised a beautiful intelligent, worldly young man in Ali and I sincerely hope that he won't be scarred too much by this experience with us. He left school, took an amazing gap year working for Australia Post and is now studying at the Queensland University of Technology.

At least for the time being, Veli has returned to Kos and is immersing himself in renovating the house and land, which includes a hundred fruit trees. We have gone 'full circle' from being not married to married to not married again and I can put my hand on my heart and say we *did* Divorce With Dignity *and* have stayed friends. In fact, when I took my 'marital bling'[37] to the jeweller and asked for it to be consolidated into one large ring "With an extra pink stone", I deliberately did *not* include my original friendship ring.

Thank goodness for staying friends because the other 'full circle' thing that's happened is I've gone from not having a daughter, to having one, to not having one and now having one again! And in 2017 I attended Zoe's wedding in Turkey. Also Veli was there. Now *that* is a miracle. Not that I attended, but that he did!

After Zoe left Australia without saying goodbye to us early in 1999, we didn't know exactly where she was. We guessed she was probably in Turkey but didn't know for sure. We didn't know what happened to her goods and chattels, much of which we had supplied. And as mentioned previously we were left to tidy up the debt we had guaranteed.

I said many times to Veli "One day she'll just knock on the door." And he always responded coldly.

After about six years we had some friends for dinner one night who knew Zoe in Weipa and asked if we'd heard from her. The universe works in mysterious ways because within minutes the phone rang and it was her! She had heard that Bernie in Cairns had been unwell and I shared that he had unfortunately passed away. I recall that she said she had studied psychology and then teaching at an

---

37   A 'Jo-ism' for jewellery including wedding, engagement, and eternity rings.

Istanbul university in Turkey and was teaching English in an international school. I was pleased that she had *finally* studied something that interested her and was doing the job she should have been doing all along. I hoped she would have a better understanding about her family but it was years before she made contact again so it was hard to tell.

We'd heard on the grapevine that she'd married and had a son, but it was about another eight years before she rang again. This time we learned that she was divorced and thinking of moving to Australia with her son Emin. Veli was still very cold and had no interest in renewing the father-daughter relationship or curiosity around being a grandfather.

I was surprised but perhaps I shouldn't have been. Even when Veli had a near death experience on 3rd October 2005, when he fell off the roof of our home, I respected his wishes for me not to make an effort to find Zoe's whereabouts.

Zoe's plans to move Down Under changed when she found new love with an Italian man called Salvatorio, so we didn't hear from her again until January 2017. I spoke with her for about forty-five minutes and felt she sounded more grounded. I shared that Veli and I had separated, the house (that she had lived in) was for sale and she wouldn't be able to call that number for much longer. The stunned silence told me that I was sharing new information with her.

Zoe asked me how she could keep in touch and asked for an email address. Within minutes she sent an email with all possible contact details; including phone numbers, address,

Facebook account and photos. My motherly instinct kicked in again and I sensed that she wanted to re-connect and have a family again before re-marrying. She was especially interested in her brother Ali, who she'd last seen when he was a baby and was now bigger than her!

I forwarded the email to Veli and Ali and sent a Facebook friend request straight away. She instantly responded so, of course, I spent some time looking at photos and becoming re-acquainted. There was a Facebook photo album for her childhood with very few images in it. As I've always been a keen 'happy snapper' and taken lots of photos, I realised I had multiple 'real' photo albums with perhaps a few hundred photos of her. After all, I was her 'mother' for all those years and I considered that part of the job description!

Despite it being late at night, I went through the albums, carefully selected and re-photographed a few dozen nice pictures of her, included a couple each of her with Veli and me. That brought back lots of memories for me too. There was the photo of New Year's Eve 1994-5 where I'm wearing the same outfit I had worn for my thirtieth birthday three weeks earlier. My 'pink party' should have been all smiles but I recall an extremely stressful disruptive scene when Zoe disagreed with my friend Shaun, who was visiting from the UK.

There were also her school formal photos and eighteenth birthday where I gave her eighteen red roses and a Waterford crystal candle holder. Her party of choice was homemade burgers for about fifteen friends and there was a funny photo of three fully dressed teenage girls sitting in the bath! There was also the fabulous (although I say so myself) cake I made which was sitting on a china plate I still use. Reminiscences.

When I created a Facebook album for her and many of the photos were 'liked' by her fiancé Salvatorio immediately, I sensed I had done the right thing. I was her mother again but I wasn't sure how far to push that.

My sister Paula was turning fifty and I had plans to visit the UK and then go to a conference in the USA in June-July 2017. I emailed Zoe to let her know I would be in Europe and gave her the option of a reunion… somewhere. She immediately invited me to stay with her, so I booked to travel to Izmir in Turkey.

It was an intense three days where she went out of her way to be the perfect host. She knew my favourite colour was fuchsia and I had fuchsia bath towels! After eighteen years there was obviously some nervousness and trepidation on both sides but we both gave and received love. It was wonderful!

Before going I had so many questions I wanted to ask but decided on a more minimalist approach and just let things unfold, *be present* and move forward rather than dwelling on the past. Zoe also asked a few questions but the only one I casually asked, during a conversation about cars, was "What happened to your car when you left?" She replied "Didn't Emily sort it?" I had no idea who Emily was so stayed quiet!

There was a family mix-up around identity papers after Zoe's son had a stay with his father, so I only actually met my *grandson* Emin the evening before leaving. I observed him to be super smart, loving and funny. The name I chose for myself was Granny Jo. I asked him if I looked like a granny and when he said "No" I thought that was perfect: a mix of reverence and humour.

Zoe had thought carefully about what we may do in our precious time together and we certainly squashed a lot in. I took gifts from Australia for everyone including Salvatorio's two teenage daughters Kara and Tazia. I was flabbergasted when, after I gave Emin, Kara and Tazia Australian caps, Zoe produced an Aussie bushman's hat complete with dangling corks – a gift from Australian friends – and *then* brought out a didgeridoo that Salvatorio started playing.

So my son-in-law-to-be from Milan in Italy, had been playing the didgeridoo for longer than he had known his Aussie-Turkish bride-to-be! I was amazed and then *they* too were surprised when Emin opened his next gift from me and it was also a didgeridoo!

Our time together was over so quickly. Zoe drove me to the airport and as we said a teary farewell, she thanked me for being a wonderful mother and giving her all her parenting knowledge. I tried to dumb this down but she was insistent. I was not surprised because in our few contacts between January and July there was a public acknowledgement on Facebook in response to my Mother's Day message to her:

> "Emin made and wrote me a beautiful Mother's Day poem/card which was a very precious gift. He's such a sweet, sensitive and loving child. As mothers I think our children reflect our parenting so I would

like to say I am a damn good mother. At the same time, what made me a good mother? Thank you Jo Hassan for taking on such a huge responsibility when you were so young yourself and thanks for doing a good job! Thanks for setting an example of how a mother should be. It requires such a balance of discipline, respect and love. Happy Mother's Day and Happy Grandmother's Day! Emin is also an indirect product of YOUR parenting. See you soon! Ali Hassan and Emin, you bring so much meaning to our lives!"

I couldn't have asked for more validation of my actions when Zoe was still a child herself. And, as an aside, I enjoyed some continuity from *my* childhood and shared with her how to 'burp' a hot water bottle as Maxie had taught me!

The universe played a part in me deciding not to go to the USA - a severe snowy winter closed schools for so many days and pushed out the school term. It now wasn't convenient to visit the friend I was staying with before the conference I was to attend – a plan that was made many months before Zoe came back into my life. I decided I could go to the conference another year and give Zoe the option of having me at her wedding which had clashed with my USA visit. She jumped at that and immediately gave me a beautiful invitation. I queried whether her mother Filomena would be there as I didn't want to cause a problem and she reaffirmed that Filomena would not go. A 'Wow' moment. In fact I learned that Filomena hadn't even attended her first wedding!

In the months between separating from Veli, selling the house, moving and completing the legal paperwork, Veli and I got along well. Robust resilience was certainly a necessary tool! I was completely open with him that I was ready to have a relationship with Zoe and shared that I'd booked the flights to visit her. He was still quite cold but I 'chipped away' at him, especially around the idea that "It's not fair that Emin won't know his grandfather".

When I noticed on Facebook that Zoe was in Kos, I knew immediately that she would have gone there to visit her father. My notion that I said so many times over the years "One day she'll be on our doorstep" happened. She knocked on his door with Salvatorio, Emin and a wedding invitation. He said he would go!

So there we were. Almost thirty years after meeting, Veli and I, just four days after becoming divorced, in Izmir, Turkey at Zoe's wedding *together*. Full circle.

Our initial meeting was on Zoe's balcony. Veli had arrived a few hours earlier by ferry and coach, and me by plane from London, then a taxi. It would be natural for both of us to have some apprehension but everything was fine. We were cordial and then proceeded to spend the next three full days together. We even had adjacent bedrooms in the hotel Zoe had booked us into!

Love is one word that describes the wedding weekend. Of course you'd say that (hopefully) about *any* wedding weekend.

This was one was *so* special though for so many reasons. Even though Zoe was very busy with plans and looking after other guests who'd come from near and far, she was still wonderful and thoughtful with me. It was lovely to do 'Mother of the Bride' type activities, like going to the hairdresser together.

Three days with Veli were lovely too. We were respectful, thoughtful and kind with one another. I assumed my usual role of taking lots of photographs, including many of us together. When I included some with him in the Facebook album, I did so happily so friends in Australia could keep up with the news. I included him gladly. He is, after all, my friend of thirty years and father of my child*ren*, for which I am eternally grateful. I wore my friendship ring for the whole trip.

And, of course, 'The Universe' had to have one last laugh. The exact date that our divorce was finalised was what would have been our 28th English village wedding anniversary!

Perhaps there is resilience in love.

Or is it love in resilience?

Full circle.

Jo's Recovery Reading and Listening

These are books that, almost a couple of decades on, are still part of my library and I remember reading as part of my journey from darkness. Several may appear very *dark* themselves but perhaps at the time, that was part of the appeal: I knew that I was reading words of someone who *really* knew what I was experiencing. Some were read several times.

Birkhäuser-Oeri, Sibylle. (1988). **The Mother: Archetypal Image in Fairy Tales.** Inner City Books.
A deep analysis of the motherly images in actual fairy tales.

Bishop, Lara. (1999). **Postnatal Depression *families in turmoil.*** Halstead Press.
My last psychiatrist Dr Tom George suggested I read this. It is a comprehensive study of PND specifically and suggestions for moving through it. He wrote the Foreword and at the

time I treasured the fact that my copy is signed by both him and the author.

Burns M.D., David D. (1980). **Feeling Good.** (1999). Avon Books.
How to overcome depression without drugs.

Chopra, Deepak. 1993. **Ageless Body, Timeless Mind.** Harmony Books.
A pioneering book about the mind-body connection including happiness and ageing.

DesMaisons PhD, Kathleen. (1998). **Potatoes Not Prozac.** (2001). Simon & Schuster Inc.
A diet plan to improve mood.

Edgson, V & Marber, I. (1999). **The Food Doctor – Healing foods for mind and body.** Collins & Brown Ltd.
A reference book about the healing properties of food. It has a chapter called "Managing Depression".

Fowler, George. (1996). **Learning to Dance Inside.** (1997). Harcourt Brace & Company.
A little book about why meditation is important, rather than how to do it. I read this several times.

Frankl, Viktor E. (1946). **Man's Search For Meaning.** (1985). Washington Square Press.
Ideas developed whilst being a psychiatrist held in Nazi death camps.

Grace, Liliane. (2006) **The Mastery Club: See the Invisible Hear the Silent Do the Impossible** 5 CD audio book. Grace Productions.
A compelling children's story about the power of your mind and 'the universe'.

Hauptberger, Sharon. (1997). **On Thin Ice.** Affinity Publishing.
Australian stories about PND.

Hollis, James. (1993). **The Middle Passage: From Misery to Meaning in Midlife.** Inner City Books.
Given that so many lead a more meaningful existence after experiencing severe disruption in the middle years, a book that proposes it shouldn't be called a 'crisis' after all!

Hollis, James. (1996). **Swamplands of the Soul: New Life in Dismal Places.** Inner City Books.
An exploration of dark places of thought and how by going there we may find our life's purpose.

Hopcke, Robert H. (1997). **There Are No Accidents.** (1998). Riverhead Books.
This book about synchronicity fascinated me. I started to believe that everything was 'meant to be' and would be all right in the end.

Jung, C G. (1961). **Memories, Dreams, Reflections.** (1995). Fontana Press.
The biography and learnings of the great psychiatrist Carl Gustav Jung.

Lawson, Nigella. (2001). **Nigella Bites.** Random House.
During one of my relapses I noticed the reference to "Potatoes Not Prozac" (see above) in the introduction to the recipe for Double Potato and Halloumi Bake. After making the recipe back in 2001, this has been a staple favourite of my family.

Peck, M Scott. 1983. **The Road Less Travelled.** Arrow Books (1990). Arrow Books.
A bestseller about love, values and spiritual growth by American psychiatrist Morgan Scott Peck.

Sachs, Judith. (1998). **Nature's Prozac *Natural ways to achieve peak mental and emotional health*.** Simon & Schuster.
Not a book to read from cover to cover but rather 'dip in' to. I used to sit in the garden and read random sections.

Sharp, Daryl. (1988). **The Survival Papers: Anatomy of a Midlife Crisis.** Inner City Books.
A book to suggest that a midlife crisis is in fact "the psyche's means of reaching for a new psychological and spiritual balance".

Sharp, Daryl. (1989). **Dear Gladys: The Survival Papers Book 2.** Inner City Books.
A follow-on to "The Survival Papers" with more detail on the recovery process.

Wolpert, Lewis. (1999). **Malignant Sadness *The Anatomy of Depression*.** Faber and Faber Limited.
A book that tries to explain in layman's terms what psychiatrists and scientists know about depression.

Woodman, Marion. (1982). **Addiction to Perfection: The Still Unravished Bride.** Inner City Books.

Whilst we want perfectionism in some areas of our lives like following the recipe for a medical drug for example, in everyday life it can be like a noose around our neck to stall and disrupt progress. This book challenges the attitudes of modern women.

Other Books Referenced

Whilst not directly related to my initial recovery from PND and PTSD, these books have been relevant to my business and life story in more recent years and are referenced in this book.

Branson, Richard. (1998). **Losing My Virginity – The Autobiography.** (2002) Virgin Books Limited.
An amazing memoir sharing dozens of stories of adversity and success in life and business.

Winfrey, Oprah. (2014). **What I Know For Sure.** Macmillan
A delightful thought-provoking collection of wisdom around emotions and values. Of particular note here is the section on 'Resilience'.

Jo's Recovery Summary

Building resilience in business and life from the Jagged Edges of PTSD... actions that worked for me that may work for you or someone important to you...[38][39]

Some activities, including these, involved others:

- Visit your general practitioner doctor early.
- Prescription medication.
- See a psychiatrist or a psychologist.
- Cognitive Behavioural Therapy (CBT) one on one and/or as part of a group therapy programme.
- Acupuncture.

---

38 *Medical disclaimer:* whilst my circumstances are described here, please consult your own doctor or health care practitioner before making any decisions about your own situation.

39 A printable version of this list is available at the website www.johassan.com/books

- Traditional Chinese Medicine (TCM).

Other activities, sometimes with the support of others, I could actually do for myself but *only* once I had made a decision to seek intervention and start the healing process. Remember that *starting* may be simply making the appointment! I was so numb that initially I wasn't able to think of these things for myself. These include:

- Listen to music.
- Walk regularly (or another preferred exercise).
- Eat healthy food, especially food that connects with your emotions.
- Drink plenty of water. Evaluate your consumption of coffee, alcohol and other 'state' changers.
- Ask for help with even simple tasks if you can't think straight.
- Meditate. And, even when not meditating remember to breath. And slow down.
- Have massages and/or facials.
- Gaze at the clouds, preferably from outdoors.
- Get plenty of sleep: go to bed earlier and have a comfortable pillow. Even if you struggle to actually *sleep* at least your body is resting. When I travel my 'comfort system' includes having a hot water bottle with me. I started doing this when I had an issue with my back and I continue because it gives me a sense of security. And that makes me feel good.

- Read either to 'escape' for example fiction or, as in my case, to 'understand' the issues around mental health disorders. For this I enjoyed learning about the psychiatrist and psycho analyst Carl Gustav Jung and some of the books I read are listed in "*Jo's Reading Recovery*".
- Make some goals, even simple ones. Have something to look forward to.
- Choose to be around positive people.
- Write. Journal. Anything. Not necessarily to re-read but to empty your head in the moment.
- Make lists of activities, especially if you're more forgetful than previously.
- Take a herbal mood enhancer.
- Smile often so your brain gets used to that and feels good about it.
- Be grateful for everything. And I really mean *everything*! Examples are saying it out loud, writing a list of 100 things you are grateful for, making and contributing to a 'Gratitude Jar'.
- Celebrate the little wins as well as the big ones.
- And lastly, wear PINK! Only kidding of course, but if you don't know what it is already, find something that makes your heart 'sing' then *do that*. Often. And try to enjoy the journey. In the end it will, hopefully, all make sense.

The reality is I don't know what 'worked' and what didn't *exactly*. I took different actions over the years as my health improved and I evolved as a person. Do what feels right for you and if you're not sure what that is right now, try some of these ideas and search out some different ones of your own. Robust resilience is worth it! Good luck.

And one final comment: if you're *not* the person who could most benefit from some help, and they are unwilling and/or unable to start the process with a health professional themselves then I suggest you make an appointment for *you*.

When my friend recommended I do this, it was truly life changing.

Cultural Translation and Other Notes

I realise that a few of my terms are 'Jo-isms' and may require translation to take you from The Village to The Wider World as a global reader. These and other information useful on the same page are contained in **Footnotes** on that page.

Background explanations and extra detail in the storyline may be found in the individual **Endnotes** below. These links and other resources may be found together at the website:

www.johassan.com/books

Endnotes

I. https://www.beyondblue.org.au/the-facts/anxiety/types-of-anxiety/ptsd
II. https://en.wikipedia.org/wiki/This_too_shall_pass
III. https://www.elementsbehavioralhealth.com/mood-disorders/situational-depression
IV. https://www.beyondblue.org.au/the-facts/depression/types-of-depression
V. https://www.beyondblue.org.au/the-facts/postnatal-depression
VI. https://en.wikipedia.org/wiki/Stiff_upper_lip
VII. https://en.wikipedia.org/wiki/Fulmer
VIII. https://en.wikipedia.org/wiki/The_Office_(UK_TV_series)

IX. https://en.wikipedia.org/wiki/International_Velvet_(film)

X. https://en.wikipedia.org/wiki/Genevieve_(film)

XI. https://en.wikipedia.org/wiki/Bert_le_Vack

XII. https://www.barbour.com/eu

XIII. https://en.wikipedia.org/wiki/International_Six_Days_Enduro

XIV. https://en.wikipedia.org/wiki/Motorcycle_trials

XV. https://en.wikipedia.org/wiki/Barry_Sheene

XVI. http://www.motogp.com

XVII. https://en.wikipedia.org/wiki/Turkish_invasion_of_Cyprus

XVIII. https://en.wikipedia.org/wiki/F%C3%A9d%C3%A9ration_Internationale_de_Motocyclisme

XIX. https://en.wikipedia.org/wiki/Snowy_River

XX. https://en.wikipedia.org/wiki/Marchioness_disaster

XXI. https://en.wikipedia.org/wiki/1989_Australian_pilots%27_dispute

XXII. https://kidshelpline.com.au

XXIII. https://marcesociety.com

XXIV. https://en.wikipedia.org/wiki/Cognitive_behavioral_therapy

XXV. https://en.wikipedia.org/wiki/Traditional_Chinese_medicine

XXVI. https://en.wikipedia.org/wiki/Carl_Jung

XXVII. https://en.wikipedia.org/wiki/ADC_Telecommunications

XXVIII. https://www.techopedia.com/definition/26175/dot-com-boom

XXIX. https://en.wikipedia.org/wiki/Dot-com_bubble

XXX. https://en.wikipedia.org/wiki/Atrial_septal_defect

XXXI. https://starlight.org.au

XXXII. http://www.todayifoundout.com/index.php/2014/10/pink-used-common-color-boys-blue-girls

XXXIII. https://www.wsj.com/articles/SB10001424053111904800304576474451102761640

XXXIV. http://www.businessinsider.com/steve-jobs-apple-fired-returned-2017-7/?r=AU&IR=T/#apple-was-founded-in-1976-by-steve-jobs-and-steve-wozniak-jobs-was-the-ideas-guy-and-handled-the-business-side-of-things-wozniak-was-the-engineering-expert-neither-young-man-had-any-experience-running-a-company-though-1

XXXV. https://www.businessinsider.com.au/thomas-edison-in-the-obstacle-is-the-way-2014-5?r=US&IR=T

XXXVI. https://businesschicks.com/life-lessons-dame-quentin-bryce

Acknowledgements

Life is a complicated web of relationships. In my PEPP® model I refer to Purpose, Energy, Pleasure and Profit but there is actually an extra "P" which is People.

Whilst I'm more than happy in my own company, I thrive in the company of others. I love having special people in my life and I am just so fortunate to have lots of those. Some have been there for my whole life – like my wonderful parents – and others for nearly my whole life like my dear sister Paula and infant school friends.

Recently I was at an event and someone said "I know them really well... I've known them for over a year" and it occurred to me, not that I didn't already know this, but how super special it is to have friends now from every stage of my life. Friends I have known for fifty, forty, thirty, twenty, ten, two years as well as friends I've had for two months.

Someone else actually said to me recently "Oh are you taking on new friends?" and that made me realise that some don't! And that's OK too.

So my point in mentioning that is that there are truly a lot of people to thank. There are a lot of names in this story that is (some of) the story of my life. A few have sadly passed away but everyone else who I was able to contact has received a copy of the manuscript and I have gone ahead with their blessing. For that I am so grateful. Some even said to me "But why did you change my name? I'm happy and proud of my relationship with you and would like my real name back please!" I have, of course, obliged and won't be identifying who they are! They know and it occurred to me that that is actually yet another "full circle".

I'm very grateful to my Author-ity Author Coach Dixie Carlton. "Full Circle" was the working title I came up with on a day when we covered her workspace in sticky notes, shuffled them around and came up with a plan. The title stuck. She helped me to identify the parts of my story (previously untold) and background as to why I (usually) understand people who are struggling in some way.

Very few people talk about post traumatic stress disorder (PTSD), especially as it hailed from a difficult step-parenting scenario after having my own baby. I decided it was time to share. It has been an extremely cathartic experience on the tail end of a stressful few years. I didn't know that when I started! Dixie has seen some tears through Skype. She probably wasn't expecting that when we started.

Once we had a draft, some special people supported me with candid feedback as beta readers. Thanks for being in that team Jenny, Kim, Bill, Wendy, Michael, Paula, Lisa, Lara and my parents.

Hermann Weise receives special recognition for still having in his files the notes I handed him on 21 June 1999. I know that I still have a copy too but, having moved house recently and having not finished unpacking, receiving a copy from him was much easier than me opening another box! We didn't scan documents in those days… I'm grateful that he is still an essential part of my mental and physical health maintenance and has smiled wryly as I have become even more pink over the years!

Recently, I have re-connected and had another cup of tea with Dr Tom George. In the first manuscript he was the only person who didn't have a pseudonym. I was delighted that when we first spoke on the phone he actually remembered me and am very grateful now that he really enjoyed the book and wrote a testimonial.

Others who I thank for reviews are Julie, Jane, Martin, Sally, Chris, Bill, Michael, Daryl, Paula, Myrna, Margie, Karen, Sam, Susan, Jenny, Peter, Shelley, Kim, Lara, Cheryl and Tanya.

I acknowledge my cover photographer Louise Williams for "going the extra mile" and reading the manuscript to understand the essence of "Full Circle". She suggested making the sparkler full circle. I suggested and took along some old drop sheets as we were using her shiny brand new studio. Thank goodness because we actually had a little fire that I stomped out with my stilettos! I wish I had thought at the time to photograph the evidence; when I did think of it the next day and contacted Louise it had already been buried in the bin under other rubbish. I didn't need that photo *that* badly to ask her to go rummaging!

Over the last few years especially I have appreciated the on-going support and encouragement of my clients who have believed in me and my mission to make "doing small business" easier. They have inspired me to keep going when I may well have changed course.

I struggle with the words to thank my son Ali for his understanding of me as I have written, and written, and written… sometimes with tears flowing. And even more I struggle with words to express my gratitude to Zoe. She has completely understood my desire (read *need*) to do this now and I hope that in my so doing, she has vicariously healed more also.

We move forward stronger with love and resilience together, having gone Full Circle after some Jagged Edges along the way.

About Jo Hassan

There is nothing typical or average about Jo Hassan. She oozes vibrancy and many people, even those older than her, have said "When I grow up I want to be you". Some friends say that they follow her on social media because they want to vicariously enjoy the life that she has.

If only they knew how it has sometimes been in the past. Jo hasn't always so publicly inspired others because in an earlier era she retreated into the numb secrecy of dark despair whilst trying to overcome postnatal depression (PND) and then post traumatic stress disorder (PTSD).

With her 'blood' family on the other side of the world none the wiser for her plight, she pushed through the gloom with the nurturing support of trusted professionals, a handful of friends who became her 'new family' and her unique toolbox of resources that she's now sharing in this book.

People today see smiling "Pink Jo" and that is a decision. Wearing pink and smiling anyway was a coping strategy to survive life that became a coping strategy to survive business as well. Jo has always lived in homes that have run small businesses so she truly appreciates the daily stretches and struggles to keep personal and business time separated.

Since 2006 Jo has shared business lifestyle strategies with small business owners so they can have more freedom too. That became Jo's passion. She understands how it is and how they think. It led her to create the PEPP® Model where Purpose, Energy, Pleasure and Profit play an important part of the decision-making process before doing anything.

More than most Jo deserves the title "The Queen of Resilience" and now, via this book and speaking, she is ready to share the back story on the back story. It's time to start the hard conversation about an unusual case of PTSD, if there is such a thing. About how the girl from the English village found herself in a culturally rich marriage, mothering a distressed teenager not much younger than herself. The journey had multiple unexpected "jagged edges" and Jo found the fortitude to push through and become the inspirational person she is today.

Jo lives in Brisbane, Australia. She loves being a Mum, connecting people, making photobooks and baking (pink) cupcakes. She enjoys travelling – especially back to The Village from whence she came. To keep fit and healthy she kicks her footbike (an adult scooter with bicycle wheels) and recently achieved a goal of going 100 km in one go which took seven hours! She wore her trademark fuchsia pink and enjoyed flamboyant fun with feather boas trailing behind her.

To connect with Jo, you'll find her at:

- www.johassan.com
- www.linkedin.com/in/johassan
- www.facebook.com/JoHassanVitalityExpert
- www.facebook.com/JoHassanVitality
- www.twitter.com/JoVitality
- www.instagram.com/johassanvitality

www.ingramcontent.com/pod-product-compliance
Lightning Source LLC
Chambersburg PA
CBHW071924290426
44110CB00013B/1468